About the Author

At sixteen years of age I joined the British Army at Shorncliffe Infantry College. I have seen active service in Northern Ireland, Angola, Kosovo and Iraq. After serving sixteen years and having been part of Special Forces I left the British Army to become a security contractor. I have worked for the United Nations in Afghanistan the British Embassy Basra, Iraq and also the American Department of Defence Baghdad, Iraq.

The Iraq Diary

Mark Roberts

The Iraq Diary

Olympia Publishers
London

www.olympiapublishers.com
OLYMPIA PAPERBACK EDITION

Copyright © Mark Roberts 2019

The right of Mark Roberts to be identified as author of
this work has been asserted in accordance with sections 77 and 78 of
the Copyright, Designs and Patents Act 1988.

All Rights Reserved

No reproduction, copy or transmission of this publication
may be made without written permission.
No paragraph of this publication may be reproduced,
copied or transmitted save with the written permission of the publisher,
or in accordance with the provisions
of the Copyright Act 1956 (as amended).

Any person who commits any unauthorised act in relation to
this publication may be liable to criminal
prosecution and civil claims for damage.

A CIP catalogue record for this title is
available from the British Library.

ISBN: 978-1-78830-161-9

This is a work of creative nonfiction. The events are portrayed to the
best of the author's memory. While all the stories in this book are true,
some names and identifying details have been changed to protect the
privacy of the people involved.

First Published in 2019

Olympia Publishers
60 Cannon Street
London
EC4N 6NP

Printed in Great Britain

Dedication

I would like to dedicate this book to all security operators and civilians who lost their lives putting themselves in harm's way while working in Iraq.

Acknowledgements

I would like to thank Stacey for standing by me through the good and the bad times.

I have seen death and suffering in my life, the two most significant memories I have are the memory of my father's death and giving medical help to a five-year-old Afghan girl blown up by a Taliban booby trap IED while I was in Afghanistan. The death of my father was an extremely painful experience, I remember clearly, as if it was yesterday, while I was working as a security adviser to the UN in the Paktika province in Afghanistan. I had a call on my satellite phone, it was my sister, a numb feeling came over me as she informed me that my father had suffered a heart attack and would never be the same person again.

I travelled home within twenty-four hours to be by my father's side not knowing what to expect or what emotions would overwhelm me. Walking through the corridors of the hospital, my stomach aching inside me and anxious thoughts running through my head, I pause and I take a deep breath. I push the ward door open and look in shock as I only see a shadow of the man my father once was, then it hits me like an emotional freight train travelling deep into my soul. I cried hard like a whimpering child, uncontrollably, and leant over his fragile body to kiss him on the forehead. My father slowly opened his eyes, smiling painfully he rolled his eyes as if to gesture, 'look at the state of me son' and no words could leave his lips as he had a breathing tube fitted to assist his breathing.

The following day at 13.03 p.m. my father passed away — did he wait for me to be at peace? I'd like to believe so. It was at this point I remember him saying to me, 'Anthony if you ever get the chance to go somewhere and do something you love then just do it son.' My mind set, I would look for the next chapter in my life and put to use the finely tuned skills I had learned while in the forces, to a job I had become attached to regardless of the risk. I would be back in a war zone, where as a security officer and where people were coming out of dictatorship whilst being overrun with insurgents. My diary gives a front seat to the placid beginnings of what would be the most difficult experiences of my life, surviving IEDs, gun battles, losing friends and the personal emotions felt during this journey. Living life on the edge never had such a truthful meaning.

26/10/06

I arrived at the Villas (Baghdad), I've been told that I'll be on the Parson's V contract which will be a security escort for HGVs carrying explosives, to destroy unexploded and disused ordinance. We were told that the company has lost a lot of guys on the Parson's V contract and that they have regular contact including small arms and EFP/IEDs (Explosive Formed Projectile/ Improvised Explosive Device). We had a brief with Jim (one of the managers at the Villas) he said that the rotation/job would be about eighteen months as that is how long the guys had lasted before showing signs of battle stress.

Bumped into one of the guys from the Afghan contract (Kenny, a Scottish lad and bubbly character ex Argyle), he will be on the Parson's V contract as well. This will be some of the other guys first contract, especially the guys who have just left the army and completed their Phoenix course. Dave is probably the oldest guy in our team, he's returned after recovering from being shot in both arms during a job north of Fallujah.

Got weapons issued, good choice there were Bushmasters, M4, M16, and AK 47s. I chose an M4, the newer version of the M16 (with 400 rounds of 5.56 ammunition) and having experience in using them in the jungles of Brunei I find it a reliable weapon, I also got issued a 9 mm Beretta for close quarter use.

27/10/06

Travelled down to Hila which is 120 kms south of Baghdad, near Babylon, this is where we'll spend the next ten days at the Armor training camp before we get deployed onto the job. The training camp is a part of land which is owned by the Kubah family and has Iraq national instructors; humorously it is also used for chicken farming. On our arrival brief, we were told that the day before our arrival an American SF soldier was killed by a large roadside IED/EFP after his convoy had left Hila training camp.

This wasn't good news especially as we were the first to have driven the route from the Villas to Hila in the last three weeks, as another team had been ambushed and EFP'd. There seems to be a lot of Fijians working for security companies over here even in Armor Group, mind they're a bit rusty with their drills and firing warning shots at cars on the way wasn't good practice, just brings attention to the team, 'What's that all about'. Arrived at Hila at lunch time, just chilled and prepped kit for next day.

Iraq National Instructors at Hila.

28/10/06

First day training today, we did weapons tests for pistol and rifle. I don't know w

hy but the day had the feel of Sennybridge training area about it (flashbacks) must be the shit-hole of a feeling giving similar vibes. The guys are OK although some are a bit rusty but they'll pick things up as they go along and there is always a good bond with the guys, a certain camaraderie.

My pistol drills give my previous SF training away as I spent most of the course pistol training hard to believe some civi Olympic pistol champ teaches the Hereford boys. I'm still wondering what this contract will be like, I know I'll have to be on my toes. People back home think I don't worry about coming out here but the risks are there and I do think, what if. I know my family are worrying but it will be hard for them to understand my passion for what I do, it's not always about the money.

Pistol Firing Test.

29/10/06

Did medic revision today, it was a bit different in the fact that it was based a lot on blood loss. Our American instructor (Dave) seemed very blasé about explaining the type of injuries we will encounter, Dave said he was over here to make money and had no previous military experience, which I found strange but if he needs the cash so be it, big risk though. We did some intravenous training on each other to give us experience on putting drips into patients, good practice though.

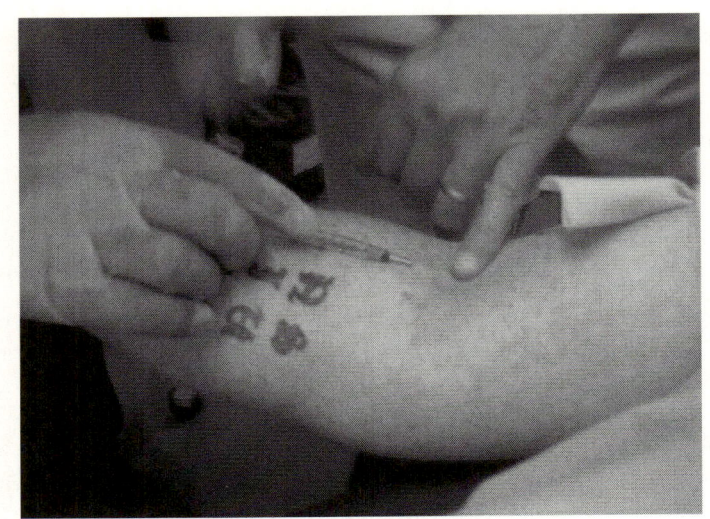

Kenny having cannula placed.

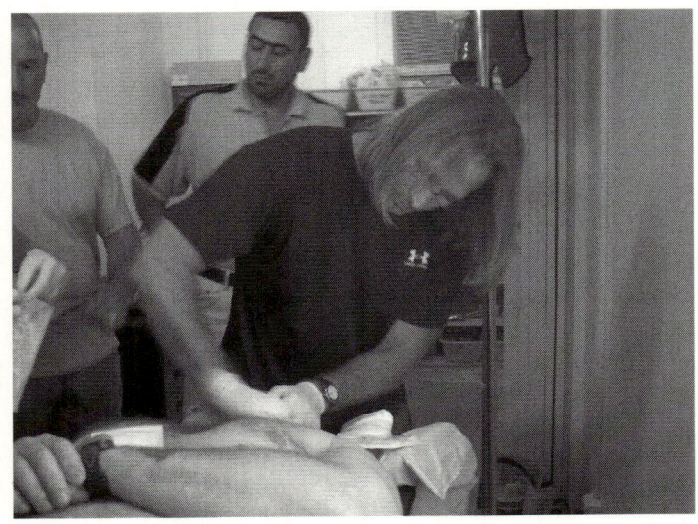

Dave (medic) putting cannula in John's neck.

30/10/06

Reasonably quiet day today, went onto the range to re-zero my weapon as we zeroed weapons at twenty-five metres, I zeroed at one hundred metres preferable distance as we won't be firing in contacts closer than two to three metres. After the range, I took Kenny and Ian through some vehicle drills as they hadn't worked in Iraq before, covered cross decking and actions on contact/ambush client control.

31/10/06

Another broken night's sleep, that's the joys of sharing a twelve-man room, it offers a wide range of sleeping patterns, like Dave's squeaky bed and then there's Kenny's snoring, which can best be compared with a low flying C130 Hercules. We had comms training with Jalal (Iraqi instructor) he went through using the HF Codan, VHF Radio and ACER PDA Track 24 Satellite System which I've already had the pleasure of using on the Afghanistan contract. It's not very effective on the move as your hands shake all over the place but useful for the panic button.

In the afternoon, we carried out some vehicle extraction training with Dave (medic). We did casualty cross decking and treating multiple casualties.

We were told by Clint (Armor Training Team Manager) that a PWC convoy vehicle was hit yesterday, mind I noticed the vehicle's panic button had been operated when we were having our comms brief. The four guys travelling in the vehicle were killed; another convoy team was travelling in the opposite direction when they were suddenly ambushed. One of their HGV vehicles crossed the central reservation and collided with an armoured car, killing all four guys inside, not good news.

Well I should have known something would happen on Halloween. Coming back from the TV room about 21:00hrs when I heard mortars landing near the compound, you never forget the cracking sound they make when they land. One didn't detonate so we'll see if it landed inside the compound in the morning. They were fired probably by the local militia from about four hundred metres away from a vehicle so they would have been fired nearly vertical, at least one of the guards took a couple of shots at the vehicle before it drove off.

Some of the guys before vehicle extraction training from left to right John, Ian, Kenny and Iraqi Guard.

01/11/06

Did some med training with Dave, concentrated on getting a clear airway on a casualty and how we may have to deal with a casualty who has had their face blown off. Dave mentioned that there had been a number of casualties where the armoured glass was blown into the vehicle and caught people in the face 'nasty'. He also said that in most bomb incidents he would not try and resuscitate the casualty as there is a ninety-nine per cent chance that their dead and a one per cent chance of survival. Lee asked, 'What if it's your mate that's been blown up, you just can't leave him and not attempt to save his life?'

Dave said, 'If it makes you feel better just so you know you tried.'

Bumped into Ritchie, he arrived today, we were working in Basra A POD where he was working for Aegis and I was working for CRG. He said he is on the PWC convoy contract, or as Ritchie calls it, Operation Certain Death. More bad news today, we were told there'd been more fatalities yesterday in Falujah; a PWC convoy was set up into an ambush. One vehicle was IED, all four inside were killed, three Iraqi's and one expat. The contact lasted one hour and thirty minutes just wondering if they had enough ammo, I hope they give us more ammo. The expat that was killed was Rab MacAllister (ex British Army) an Irish guy who I met on my way over here, he was returning from four weeks leave, I bet he never saw it coming, my thoughts are with his family.

02/11/06

My phone alarm went off this morning at 7am and I realised we have a thief in our room; he's furry and two inches long — bloody mice everywhere. I looked over to turn my alarm off and the mouse jumped out of my kit bag. I'd left a ration pack temptingly open and he'd been tucking in quite nicely and covered most of my kit with its contents. Funny enough, the

Afghan mice have a liking for chocolate powder. I've sealed my kit but I have a suspicion that he's going to move onto Ritchie's kit tonight, the little fucker.

Went for a run with Ritchie and Ian this afternoon, we discussed our role over the next few weeks and the harsh reality that one of us may be killed. It seems strange to talk of death but it's part of the job we will be doing and could come at any time, I just hope it doesn't come my way and my father is doing his bit by watching over me. Been missing Charmaine and Nico today, I wish Michelle would have let me see them before I left for Iraq, it's those little things that keep you going in the hardest days when you are filled with sadness and worry.

03/11/06

Well Ritchie didn't sleep too well as he needed regular visits to the toilet as he's got a good case of the shits, not very surprising as the cooks and kitchen helpers never wear gloves and I know they don't wash their hands regular. I suppose wiping their arse with their left hand instead of toilet paper doesn't help, I'd say it's more of a splash and rub 'nice'.

Went to the little Iraqi shop and asked the shopkeeper to get me a leg pistol holder. I've noticed it's harder to barter with Iraqis than Afghans. Somehow Afghans seem more submissive than the Iraqis. Their level of cooking is something to be desired, Iraqi's just deep fry everything and cook the same food every day, oh for the delights of the choice of food back home, mmm.

Met Darren McKenzie today we were in the same team for CRG at Basra A POD, he said he resigned on leave as the pay is shit. Darren is in his early forties and was a former New Zealand

SAS soldier, mind he finds a lot of relief now in his strong belief in God but I need to see more miracles before I'm converted.

Ian and I went to have a look at a damaged vehicle that had sustained an EFP hit. It's a very effective form of attack which has been introduced to Iraq by the Iranians. Plastic explosive is placed behind a disk/circular piece of copper or brass and is initiated by an infrared beam which the vehicle breaks to cause the explosion. A slug or missile is formed by the blast travelling at 5,000 mph and penetrates vehicle armour easily; it has been the biggest cause of death and injury this year.

Effect of Homemade EFP twelve inch diameter plastic bottle filled with C4 plastic explosive, slug has penetrated straight through driver's armoured door.

On the inside of the door it's clear to see the slug has gone through the door and driver's seat, exiting through the passenger side door, it would have killed the driver instantly.

Just been informed by Clint, that a local man who was training to become part of the Iraqi equivalent of the SAS was beheaded by local militia today, his body was brought back to the village. That would explain the gunfire we could hear earlier, Clint said there is trouble brewing in a village north of Hillah and to be on standby tonight, 'here we go'.

04/11/06

Well, our alarms went off a bit early and louder this morning in the form of six mortars, their cracking thud was unmistakable, also with a bit of small arms gunfire for good measure, getting dressed in the dark was a giggle. Conrad went to turn the light on which would have been good for the close-range spotter to mark on but a quick shout of, "Don't put the fucking light on," changed his mind. We could hear one of the guards opening up in the general direction of where the mortars were being fired from, he fired around three hundred rounds, another guard was startled and decided to start firing as well, in the wrong direction towards a village, nice one. A number of unexploded mortars were found so I think Clint is going to get the EOD guys to come and do a controlled explosion to sort it out.

I like Clint's calm collected approach to the attacks it's quite amusing the way he comes in and says, "Good morning lads," and then begins to explain the events of the attack as if describing what he had for lunch in a blasé manner.

Unexploded mortar beneath tyres surrounded by razor wire, our accommodation in the top right of the picture.

We'll probably be here for another two days as there's a curfew due to Saddam Hussein's verdict in court tomorrow; there is a high risk of trouble, so no movement.

Got bad stomach cramps today, Ian has been in bed all day and has been looking pretty shit.

05/11/06

I think Kenny and Ian are having trouble sleeping because they're like a pair of sparrows in the morning. I think Ian may be a little uneasy about going out on the job especially after being shot twice. Kenny is new to the Iraq thing and doesn't really know what to expect but the only thing you can do is wait to get out on the ground as that is where the experience is gained from the people you work with and the scrapes you get into.

On the range firing the Minimi, Kenny in the background.

Did some Minimi shooting, it's a 5.56mm machine gun used as our main support weapon, it's a reliable weapon but if you have to use it then the shit has really hit the fan.

Just heard on the local news that Saddam Hussein has been sentenced to death by hanging for his first conviction.

06/11/06

Well we heard some bangs tonight thinking it was thunder as there have been a lot of storms lately but we were told by Clint that a number of Catusha rockets were fired at the American Embassy and the American Special Forces Base, there was one SF soldier injured. We'll all be leaving for the Villa's tomorrow to do the change-over so the other teams can go on leave, it'll be nice to crack on with the job and get busy.

We were given our 'Rules for the use of Force' cards; probably the most important part is the 'Use of Deadly Force' paragraph three which says you can use necessary force up to and including deadly force, against persons in the following circumstances:

- In self-defence.
- In defence of facilities, persons, as specified in your contract
- To prevent life threatening offences against civilians
- In defence of coalition – approved property specified in your contract.

Let's hope we don't have to use deadly force too much, unless we have to but I can honestly say, 'Seeing the way the militia easily behead people I wouldn't even blink before the round has passed through his head'.

07/11/06

Well I've seemed to have made a friend in the little mouse who has taken residence in our room, I'm sure he knows we're moving out today. He slept on my desert combat grab bag last night; he soon woke up when I began to get my kit ready. The guys were chasing him around the room but I told them not to harm him even though he had a shit on my bag.

I sense a little tension in Ian and Kenny, they know this won't be like the Afghan contract and it will be a little livelier. It's confirmed now that we'll be moving up to the Villas today around lunch time.

Got to the Villas around lunch time, as we left Hillah earlier than expected, we had no incidents on the way up from Hillah. After arriving we went to the PX, you can always count on the Americans to have everything like Burger King, Pizza Hut and a Subway sandwich bar, they never do things in half measures, although it was nice to get some food shopping in as I'm fed up of MREs already.

I found out earlier that Eric has resigned; Eric said he had spoken to his wife and with the added pressure of being on the PWC contract, it just seemed too much of a risk for him. Eric will be flying out to Kuwait tomorrow, he'll be lucky if he is offered another job with Armor. I went to exchange my helmet earlier and while I was in the stores, me and some of the other lads noticed Rab's box and some of his belongings along with some paperwork which was waiting to be sent back to his family. It seems strange to think his kit is going home without him and that nearly two weeks ago he was home with his family, 'The risks we take'.

08/11/06

Got a text early this morning from my Kiwi butty, Dave, he's stuck at Kuwait airport due to flight problems. Dave said he should be back at the Villas tomorrow. We got five more mags of ammo issued and radios today ready for our first op, which will probably be on Thursday.

The PSD guys left for Camp Victory and the Farm today, so said farewell to John and told him to keep his head down, Kenny volunteered for a vacant slot in the PSD team but I'm not sure how well he'll cope with the job. He hasn't any experience in close protection work before but hopefully he'll be OK. I've seen some signs of irritation amongst the guys already and it's early days yet, that's one of the things with living in cramped and close proximity of one another you just have to get on.

We received our food allowance money today so I got some supplies from the local shop. I asked Salam (Iraqi guard working for Armor) to collect it for me as his sentry point is opposite the shop. I laughed at the device he used to collect the goods — a long length of phone cable with an empty sandbag attached to the end of it, simple but effective.

Clint arrived up at the Villas today ready to go on leave tomorrow and will be leaving with a bang, on his way in, his team was hit with a remote controlled IED in the form of two 155mm artillery shells. There were no casualties just a bit of shrapnel damage to Clint's vehicle; obviously their vehicles had been watched as they were driving in towards the Villas.

Did some running and weight training this afternoon, always helps to keep in shape out here as it makes carrying the kit a little bit easier "Men sano en corp sano", healthy mind in a healthy body.

I watched a film at lunchtime today it was a remake of *The Alamo*, I felt a little saddened watching the film as it made me think where we are going in the world. People centuries ago, and in our century today, have been fighting wars, some wars I've been involved in while I was in the army makes me think where all this violence is taking us. People in the real world are so oblivious to the ripples caused by someone getting killed out here, that person's family will be left with memories and an empty void with little answers about what really happened to their loved one. I'm just a small fish in the pond of life.

Roof tops of Baghdad, smoke can be seen rising from a previously exploded IED left of picture above trees.

09/11/06

Lots of gun fire last night so there must have been a lot of insurgent activity, moved all our kit into the Convoy Villa this morning so all the teams are together.

We've been given the task of collecting the bodies of some of the guys who were ambushed in Falujah including Rab's body.

Went with George "Kiwi" (Team Leader) up to the American camp, journey was relatively good and it was my first time as gunner on the Minimi. It was a bit windy so I made sure I had my shamag over my face and gloves on, it seemed a lot colder up north. We got to Falujah just after lunch and made use of some MREs yum, George went with an American lieutenant to be shown where to collect the bodies from, probably a cooler Iso container.

I don't think anything prepares you for seeing someone's lifeless body in a typical long, black body bag. There were four body bags in total two Iraqi's, Rab's and a body bag with what they cleared up from the seen, as they couldn't distinguish whose parts was who's. George and some of the guys started to put the bodies into the back of his vehicle. One the Iraqi's was quite a large figure so they had to sit the bag upright as if he was riding his last journey home. They laid Rab across the back seat, he was missing the lower part of his body and had lost his left arm and the other Iraqi, well what was left of him, fitted nicely into the footwell of the vehicle as there wasn't much left of him, then finally the body bits.

We brought the bodies back down to Baghdad where the Iraqi bodies will be given to their families and Rab's will be flown back to Ireland. I think you can't put a price on life but I wonder what Rab's family will feel when they get $250,000 instead of him, not very happy I expect.

Got back to the Villas and was told that one of the teams had been hit by an IED, no casualties luckily. Teams seem to be getting hit every other day at the moment, don't these bastards ever have a day off, or sleep, what hatred drive them to such extreme measures?

The Convoy/PSD Villas.

Conrad, John, Rob and Lee taking some time out watching TV.

10/11/06

Fucking fuming, as Aussie, one of the TLs, came in last night and said they need three guys to go onto PLS, which is transporting C4 high explosives in HGV trucks. Ian and another lad put their hands up and volunteered and my name was picked out of the hat. What Ian and Garry don't realise, is they'll be truckers travelling at a maximum speed of 58mph which is shit if something goes wrong, 'vaporised I'd say'. They both volunteered and they haven't a clue what they've volunteered for.

We were taken up to the Farm, which is a big coalition complex mostly American military, here we will do some vehicle familiarisation. I'm not happy as I could earn £400 a week back home driving trucks and come home alive and this wasn't in the contract agreement I signed in London with Bex. I told Jim (PLS manager) that I would try it out and if it seems OK I'd stay but otherwise I'll move on, Jim said, "Well we're here to do as we're told." Bollocks this isn't the army and they should have someone who has no Iraq experience driving the HGVs. I've got previous Iraq experience so the logical thing to do is get me on the ground with the Parsons V Team where I belong.

I'll just have to see how it goes and I know the choices I make out here will determine whether I put myself in harm's way, there are always risks. I'll be on the internet tonight scoping for a new job by the looks of things, 'same shit different place and company'.

11/11/06

Did first day of driving today, I was bored out of my brain and doing first parade on the PLS is more or less the same as the Leyland drops. I had spent a lot of time driving Drops vehicles when I was in Germany and was familiar with loading and unloading. I was told that after I'd completed the training I would be going back to the Villas to join the convoy team again, 'excellent'.

Camp Victory is your typical American type base with shops; main PX and food bars all over the place and each soldier must have his own Humvee. I spent most of the evening in bed not feeling well at all, regular toilet visits and my body is aching all over. That is a big problem here, hygiene, just the simplest of things like not washing your hands out here can give you a knock and you'll be ill for a few days.

I spoke to Kenny and he said he isn't too keen on doing the PSD work, he asked if he could take my place but it was too late, oh well live and learn. I'm really looking forward to tomorrow's training, I just wish the next couple of days would fly by.

PSD vehicles heavily armoured to ensure clients safety.

12/11/06

Continued with the PLS training today, practising loading and unloading an explosives container, I was unable to do the training in the afternoon as I had a relapse in my stomach pains it must be a super bug.

Got our last day tomorrow yippee and then I'm off back to the Villa's, Danny and Ian said Rodger Bannister will be coming round to visit later as he's over here working with CRG. Rodger was one of the managers on the Kroll Afghanistan job; he was formerly Argyle Regiment but did ten years with the SAS. I think he's still embarrassed what happened at Kroll house in Kabul, he pulled a Mouser pistol out of his drawer in his room and fired it off by accident. Rodger shot himself in the hand, the bullet went straight through his hand and went through Andy Gibson's leg 'ouch', then got lodged in the wall, shortly after, he was removed from country, didn't look good for an ex SAS soldier but accidents happen. Will be going to bed early as it's the only time I feel comfortable and the TV room does my head in, bloody American soldier propaganda TV makes me feel sick. Danny told us that Saddam Hussein is in a secured prison compound on the Victory Base, you know when he is in court as the streets are crowded with US tanks.

PLS vehicle with explosives container.

13/11/06

Well I feel a lot better today but still have the odd stomach cramp now and then. I was able to visit the Defrag (American cookhouse) for the first time and have a good look around. It's amazing what they have — there're two hot plates with different menu's, salad bar, stir fry bar, curry bar, burger bar, kebab bar and every other food you can think of and there's no limit just take what you want. The sweets and afters are cake bar, ice-cream bar, fresh fruit bar, smoothies and every drink imaginable, by the time you've made your mind up you have to go back to work.

It's just good old tyre changing tomorrow then that's it for Ian and Garry, I'm being picked up by Team 47 when they come and back to the Villas. Done a bit of last minute shopping as it's more reliable than the choggy shop outside the Villas, check e-mails later then hit the sheets.

14/11/06

Yippee finished the PLS training at the Farm got picked up by my team in the afternoon then was brought back to the Villas. It was nice to see Dave (Kiwi) again, the last time we were both hung-over after a great night out in Swansea. He said he would try and get me into his team but I won't hold my breath though, even so, it would be nice as since I've come back I've found some of the guys aren't happy with some of the team members and one lad has said he may resign.

It was clear why they were unhappy, I found out that the team 2i/c had got the team lost and driven them out of the Green Zone and lead them into the Red Zone. One of two things can happen if you make that mistake you either lose your head or drive straight into an ambush and get greeted with RPGs (Rocket Propelled Grenades).

Well I think it best to sit this rotation out and see where we go from here; there will always be other contracts in other places.

It seems a little strange to be back at the Villas and I've left a lot of comforts behind at Camp Victory, It's a beautiful place in a sense and to think it was Saddam's palace seems hard to believe. The public were forbidden from coming anywhere near his palace grounds during his dictatorship/reign and the man-made lakes were impressive, I wonder if water is a show of wealth.

There was good security at camp Victory and the sound of a near bomb going off tonight reminds me of that and the fact of the Shark Eye device. They have balloons attached to wire held at about 1,000 feet and beneath it is a surveillance camera called Eagle Eye, it can see all around up to twelve kilometres and read out of a note book at that distance, it's so precise for the cost of three million pounds I should think so.

Well stomach is still playing up and I'm beginning to think I'll have the longest case of the shits, ever even after taking medicine. Off up to Camp Victory tomorrow to the Farm to do some more medic training but it's all good I suppose as you never know when you'll need to use it.

Saddam's Palace at the left the picture, one careful owner.

Balloon with Eagle Eye attached beneath.

15/11/06

Dave (Kiwi) had an interesting day as a TL on his first day, he came into a contact up near Falujah. Dave said it was like the scene out of *Saving Private Ryan* where they're on the beach, there were rounds landing everywhere. They came under fire by machine gun PKMs and RPG, one of the rear vehicle gunners was shot in the back of the head, the lads tried to save him but there wasn't anything they could do. He died after as a result of the fatal bullet wound, his name was Mesa, a Fijian guy. Dave said they were attacked on the way back to camp Victory as well, that would explain why we were put on standby to go out and help as we were at Camp Victory at the time. I met a member of Dave's team who comes from Penrhos, Wayne James, he's five years younger than me and I can't remember him from back home but it was nice to meet a local lad out here.

Our call sign towed Dave's damaged vehicle back to the Villas, it was covered in bullet holes. I drove the damaged F350 vehicle and Lee was my passenger, we did get a little bit worried by being towed through Baghdad at 100kph and at a distance of about five metres. When I got back, I saw Dave leaving the Fijian's accommodation, so he had obviously been to see how the lads were, it was nice to see he was OK.

Heard a long gun battle earlier this evening, so the militias are feeling confident tonight, hoping to have a quiet day tomorrow and get my overnight kit ready for Al Asad which means we'll be passing Falujah so we'll need to be on our toes.

16/11/06

Haven't been out today, which is a good thing as I've heard around seven loud explosions nearby and on in the last half hour.

There has been a lot of gunfire today and around lunchtime just a hundred metres down the road outside the Villa's.

I was told by Dave, that the Fijians are refusing to work unless they get a pay rise, They are on £1,500 a month which is terrible compared to our £6,300 but that's the main reason most guys are out here, hired guns for good money if you can put a price on your life. The Fijians also want their vehicles to have better protection on the gunners position as they are quite open compared to our closed pods with the gunners hatch.

Well the Fijians are taking a few days off to mourn their lost comrade so we'll just have to see what happens.

We've still had no news on whether there are any jobs on tomorrow so it's just sit tight and guess, mind the briefings are non-existent so I'll check my crystal ball later. Did a bit of weight training in the gym but didn't push it too hard as I am slowly but surely trying to recover from this stomach bug.

Just been told that me and four other lads have got to stand in for the Fijians, so I'll be joining Dave's team tomorrow, going up north to all the nice places 'not', so I'll be on my toes tomorrow. My dad needs to be doing his guardian angel bit and covering my arse; we'll be leaving at 8am and possibly staying out overnight.

17/11/06

Got up nice and early this morning, welcomed by a brew made by Bob then when we went over to meet Dave. We were told the run up to Tikrit and further north was delayed by twenty-four hours so we should be going tomorrow if there is no change. The other guys went up to FOB Falcon and returned by lunchtime with no incidents. We've heard that 'Crescent', (American Security Company), have had a PSD team (eight pax) kidnapped today, they pulled up to a checkpoint where insurgents were wearing IP (Iraq police) uniforms. When they stopped, one of the insurgents managed to get the driver's door open on one of the vehicles and drew a pistol on the occupants. You never unlock your doors outside a secure compound, its much safer to do hand signals from behind the bullet proof glass. The Americans should have shown some force and attempted to shoot the gunman and drive off. I can't imagine seeing them alive again, I would prefer to get killed attempting to get out of that situation rather than lose my head.

The Iraqi Army had twenty Humvee's stolen today so there might be a new garage opening up in down-town Baghdad, Hummers for sale, they come with free explosives, how can you lose twenty Humvees — only in Iraq.

Got a picture off Gary earlier, he's had a lot of experience out in Iraq and is hoping to leave shortly for either an Afghan or Nigeria contract. The picture he gives me was of Uday Hussein's (Saddam's son – killed 2003, Mosul) lions. During Saddam's reign, Uday would get his men to kidnap a young girl from off the streets in Baghdad then he would rape them then give her to his men, then they would throw the girls into the lions cage to be eaten. When the coalitions forces came into Iraq, they managed to send some of the young cub lions to the Berlin zoo but the lions, who had tasted human flesh, had to be put to sleep unfortunately.

Gary, eye to eye with one of Uday Hussein's lions, unfortunately it was one of the lions that had to be put to sleep.

18/11/06

Things always start as they mean to go on and not being able to find the keys to one of the vehicles was a good sign something was going to happen, this morning I joined Team 41 on a Parsons Convoy pickup at ASB 3. I was commander of vehicle three my role was to keep the convoy packed tight and check gaps, we would be travelling up through Sammarra then past Tikrit. On our team, as well was Phil (team leader second vehicle), Steve (point vehicle), Padge (rear vehicle) and myself in the third vehicle, we also had Fijian drivers and top gunners.

We went to meet the convoy at camp Victory at around 9am, there were ten vehicles, one carrying a crane, two low loaders, two tractor units without loads and the rest flat beds. Baghdad was busy today and no doubt a quick mobile phone call from a spotter informed the insurgents we were on our way up north even from the IP or INGs.

My driver is Marika (Fijian) he was polite enough to give me a running commentary on all the hot spots on route, which was most of the journey. There were dead dogs everywhere on the roads as many as hedgehogs back home, Marika said the Mosul road was a good ambush site and with the bushes and railway bank I'd agree.

At around 10am we got to an ING checkpoint as we began to slow down. I noticed the ING soldiers back against the blast wall to take cover, it was at this point I heard Llatia (Fijian top gunner) shout 'contact' as we were taking gun fire from the rear. I told Marika to drive away from the checkpoint out of the line of fire.

We continued on the north road for about one hour thirty minutes, I noticed the convoy had spread in the middle. I told Marika to drive alongside vehicles four, five, six so that I could give hand signals to the drivers in order to close the gaps. Shortly after this, near Sammarra 10 kms away, from ASB 3 at around 11:30am I noticed the third flatbed vehicle starting to sway and break away from the convoy, the flatbed seemed to just pull off the road and park. At first I didn't think it was one of our vehicles as I couldn't figure out why it had pulled over and stopped.

I told Phil, over the radio, what had happened and that I was going to check the vehicle. I approached the cab of the flatbed carefully. At first it seemed as if there was nobody in the vehicle, Padge and I joked that the driver had either gone for a piss or a cup of coffee. I tried to open the driver's door but it was locked, the driver's window seemed open so I went to look inside the cab. As I peered over the driver's door I could see fragments of flesh and skull on the steering wheel and also the driver slumped down in the footwell of the vehicle.

I called for a response from the driver but knew he was dead and didn't even bother checking for a pulse from the state of his motionless body. I shouted to Padge, "He's been shot," and ran my hand across my throat to indicate that he was dead. At that point, a chill went down my spine as I knew there was a sniper in the area and I didn't want to be the next victim. Steve came to assist with the vehicle while Padge blocked the road to prevent traffic travelling through. ING soldiers also came to assist in removing the driver's body from the cab which they tried to do miserably and there was no way I was going to get scarlet all over my beige kit.

We didn't have a body bag on us so we had to use one of the Fijians sleeping bags, we then placed the driver's body in the back of Steve's vehicle, there's no dignity in death and I felt a little sorry for cramping the driver's body in the back. I got another driver to get the vehicle as he would need to drive it down to the main convoy. I was impressed with the ease at which the Philippine driver just jumped in the blood stained cab even though I told him the other driver had been shot and killed. We loaded the blood-stained vehicle onto one of the low loaders and put another unit onto the flatbed to continue with the journey up to ASB 3. Apache air cover came over us for the rest of our journey, we had to take the body to camp Striker to keep him in the morgue (refer unit).

During this time, we dropped the driver off at the morgue, the American soldier working at the morgue identified the driver from the passport that was found on him, his name was Abid Hussein. We'll collect Abid's body from the morgue in the morning before we make our way back to ASB 3 to collect the convoy for the return journey.

Where Abid's flatbed came to a stop after he was shot.

ING's attempting to remove Abid's body.

Me and my driver, Marika.

19/11/06

It was cold last night and sleeping in a transit tent with no heating doesn't help, chorus snoring from the Fijians was an added extra. Got up at around 5.30 a.m. to go for a shave and clean up, then went to breakfast at the Defrag, we collected Abid's body from the morgue around 7.30 a.m. then drove round to the car park as we had to wait for the US Forces to clear the route south of any IED's. Phil, Padge and Steve went to the 'Green Bean café', to get their fix of caffeine while I stayed with the vehicles; the Fijians are very religious and had a church gathering prior to us leaving. Niko led the service while the others sung along, I found their singing very soothing and quite emotional. After they had finished, they shook hands with one another including me and said, "God Bless You."

We headed back down to meet the convoy at ASB 3 then set off south for Baghdad, as we passed the site where Abid was shot, I made constant glances to either side of the convoy to make sure the vehicles were OK. The drivers take an incredible risk to drive these lorries but I've noticed that they have all taken precautions today and are wearing their body armour and helmets.

It was a quiet drive all the way down until we were told that another call sign had been in a contact where some small arms had been fired at them, so we would have to be careful. We had an idea, it would probably be at the ING checkpoint where we had been shot at yesterday. After driving through the ING checkpoint we passed coalition forces sweeping for IEDs, about five minutes after this I heard Steve shout 'contact', as we were at the rear of the convoy, I knew we would come into the killing zone soon. I could suddenly hear automatic gunfire coming from my right, I said to Marika, "There the bastards are, in the field by the bush line." The smoke rising from their weapon was clearly visible. It was a comforting sound to hear Llatia (Fijian gunner) open fire with the Minimi machine gun from the back of our vehicle and he must have got over a hundred rounds off in the direction of the insurgents.

Fijian gunners Llatia (left) and Mijieli (right) with Minimi machine gun.

We kept driving and finally got out of contact and continued with our journey down to Camp Victory in Baghdad. When we arrived, Abid's body was given to a Parson's representative in order for them to prepare his body to be sent back to Pakistan. After dropping off the convoy, I went for a well earned Burger King, then headed back to the Villa's. When I got back, everyone asked how I was and seemed interested in what happened and with a lot of the guys doing the same journey tomorrow they were a little edgy after hearing what happened to our convoy. I was told later in the evening, by Phil, that intelligence reports confirmed that two insurgents were killed when Llatia returned fire.

Good cover for insurgents to set an ambush, this picture was taken near the area where we came under fire.

20/11/06

It was nice to have a lie-in this morning and the guys left early so I hope they had an incident free run up north. Give my M4 and Berretta a good clean, went to the gym in the afternoon. I've noticed Rocket, our adopted pet, has taking a liking to John's bed, mind, she's a beautiful dog just a little dusty but friendly. If the door to our room is shut it isn't long before you can hear scratching and as soon as the door is opened it always goes for John's bed.

Well I haven't been told if I'm on a job tomorrow, I feel a bit of a floating team member at the moment not knowing what team I'll be in next but that's what happens when you put too many guys in one team overflow. I got told by Shane tonight that I'll be joining his PSD team until further notice; we'll be doing security for the Parsons clients. We're going up north on Wednesday so we're going to be guaranteed a contact, we'll just have to wait and see but I'll be on top gunner so it'll be interesting.

Rocket in her favourite position.

21/11/06

I've just been in the Villa today, will be going up north tomorrow so looks like we'll be getting hit a few times. Team 47, my original team, had four contacts on the way up yesterday and three contacts today including RPG (Rocket Propelled Grenade) attack, small arms fire and an IED. Bob was one of the gunners and he said he got some good shots on to one of the insurgent's fire positions.

I've been told by Shane that I'll be driving tomorrow, not so bad as its one of the most important jobs as you have the crew's life in your hands and will need to be aware of IEDs and EFPs. Everyone wants to be a gunner just to get some rounds off it's like a kindergarten, won't be so keen when sniper rounds start cracking over their heads.

Got a parcel off Hannah today which was my long awaited Tetley teabags and rechargeable batteries, these Lipton teabags are killing me so I'll be sticking the kettle on after I finish today's diary input.

There was a lot of gun fire outside the Villas around 5:30pm and some explosions. didn't get any information on what was going on so no need to worry I suppose.

22/11/06

Today started well really, as our journey up to Bayji went without incident except for one poor Iraqi truck driver we passed. His truck had set off a compression plate IED and blown his truck up; it must have caught fire immediately, mind, the blast would have killed him instantly. The thing I noticed the most, was the strong smell of his burning corpse, it had a familiar smell to it but I could only compare it to burning bacon, horrible I know.

After the burning truck, we carried on with our journey to Camp Buck Master where we dropped our client off then headed for Camp Spiker to collect another client to bring back down to camp Victory.

It was quiet on the way back and we received no small arms fire or RPGs but things would change as we got into the red area. As we passed Samara, I noticed some Iraqi police had found a body beside the road, I think it would have probably been an execution and they'd just dumped the body there.

Me and Paul had been discussing how the insurgents placed compression plate IEDs on the verge of the road where the gravel is; as this makes it easier to disguise them, but they have been known to put them in potholes in the middle of the road. A couple of moments later we went over a pothole, a little larger than a dinner plate, and I pointed it out to Paul then 'boom', there was a shudder as our vehicle was hit by the shockwave. I looked in my wing mirror and could see Baz's vehicle engulfed in a cloud of smoke and his driver struggling to control the vehicle, it was a remote IED which had been set off by an insurgent who was probably sitting pretty in the bushes. We were a five-vehicle convoy, I was in the fourth and Baz was in the fifth, they always go for the last vehicle mind the 350s V8 are fast for 5 – 8 ton vehicles and we were doing about 90mph, they can take a good hit as well.

We all have noticed that some of the IEDs are placed near the IP checkpoints, we know the IPs have some involvement with the insurgents and the police system is corrupt beyond belief so it wouldn't surprise me. I asked Baz and Rob if they were OK, they just seemed a little shook up. We laughed after discussing what happened and said it isn't the first and won't be the last time someone will be IED, at least they're all OK.

Jabal Hamrin mountain range in the distance north of Bayji.

23/11/28

There was a lot of gun fire this morning and some loud bangs, later we found out on BBC Internet News that over a hundred people had been killed at the Ministry of Health offices in Baghdad as it was attacked by insurgents. It's the same now as it was in the army — you'd get more information from the news than you would through your own intelligence resources, ridiculous.

Been feeling a bit low today as I've been contemplating my future and what I want out of life before it's too late. I know I can't do this forever as your luck will run out some time with or without a guardian angel, I don't really worry about myself, its who I'll leave behind and how they will feel that concerns me.

My children, Charmaine and Nico, my mother, David and my sisters. I would hate to leave a gap in their lives and cause them pain; I miss them all so much. I spoke to Denice (sister) this afternoon and felt relieved to hear a familiar voice; I spoke to my mum as well but noticed concern in both their voices.

Part of my heart wishes to be home with friends and family doing normal day to day things but the other part is glad to be here doing this job as it feels part of me. I'll try and work until next summer when the contract ends and then I will stay home. I have to settle sometime and feel comfortable back home otherwise I'll just be going around in circles never stopping.

Still no news on any jobs so it looks like we'll be sitting tight for a couple of days, we haven't heard from Team 47 either and they were meant to get back today so I hope things are OK.

24/11/06

All the guys from Team 47 got back OK today without incident, they arrived back at the Villas about lunchtime, there is still a lot of sectarian violence and we heard that six people were burnt alive today in Baghdad. The violence seems to be getting worse and there has been a big increase in attacks and bombings in the last few days.

We've been told by Shane that we won't be going out on a job until the 27th November so we'll have plenty of wind-down time. I did my usual training session this afternoon while some of my team went around to the green zone to get some shopping in at the PX. Rocky was a bad dog today as she killed the ginger kitten, some of the guys weren't happy but that's cats and dogs and it seems more natural than the human death that's happening at the minute.

Going to watch a film on Sky later and check my e-mails before going to bed, never know we might have a fast ball and have a job.

25/11/06

It's been a quiet day today and not much in likes of loud bangs and gunfire although there was a loud explosion at the green zone PX which may have been a suicide bomber. It gets pretty difficult in the Villa when both teams are in, everyone is on top of each other and people get irritated quickly. There are a lot of young lads (in middle, late 20s) who seem to have found their feet too quickly and get a bit loud and as they have only just left the army, are still only just learning the role of the close protection business for real, too cocky too mouthy. Its best to keep the mouth shut, eyes and ears open, and look in to what the older lads are doing and maybe they'll learn something.

Off out on a job tomorrow north of Al Asad to Camp Wolf, not sure what the job will entail at the moment but we should be getting a brief from Shane at the Farm tomorrow morning. Wales lost to New Zealand 45 – 10 but it was nice to watch the boys on Sky makes home feel a little closer even though they lost.

26/11/06

I've come to believe that Baz is having a bad luck streak, we went to Camp Victory nice and early for breakfast and to collect the excursion vehicle. After breakfast we went to the hotel to collect seven clients, the hotel is situated at the far side of Camp Victory. As we were heading out of Camp Victory I heard Baz shout over the radio, stop, stop, stop, he said he'd lost one of his wheels off his vehicle. It was luck that Baz lost the wheel in Camp Victory and not doing 90mph down the motorway, otherwise it could have been a different story.

The front right-hand wheel had fractured and come off, Baz's vehicle has been IEDd twice, once on the right hand side and the other at the rear. I think the blast on the right side of the vehicle had stressed the wheel; the vehicle had cracked windows as well as body damage and really shouldn't have been used as it has been weakened and may not survive another direct hit. We stripped Baz's vehicle down and took the codan off the vehicle; this meant we went from five vehicles to four.

On the way up north, I went in the pod of the third vehicle as gunner with Mick (ex 1 Para) taking turns on the Minimi doing top cover. Our journey was going well until we caught up with an American CF convoy with around one hundred and forty vehicles which slowed us right down, this believe it or not wasn't a bad thing as they were now clearing the route for us so if there were any IEDs they would set them off.

As we travelled up route Uranium, which was a single-track road, I couldn't believe how many IED blast holes there were in the road, every single bit of the way was littered with debris from vehicles that had been blown up by the pressure plate IEDs. There was mostly burnt out shells of convoy vehicles, mostly trucks and one could only imagine the quick death the driver would have suffered but there was also the odd car which meant there was the occasional passer-by who would have been caught by the blast and the IED does not choose its victim, it detonates when pressed.

The route was ideal for ambush attacks from insurgents as it is so isolated and there were signs of this with the scattered RPG fins over the ground. After we dropped our clients off, after a trouble-free run, we headed for the US Army base at Al Asad which is in the middle of nowhere. It must have been an Iraqi air base in its time as there were MIG fighter jets all over the area, some damaged or burnt out and destroyed.

Going to bed early tonight, hopefully we'll have a quick drive down route Uranium back to Baghdad tomorrow. I went outside the transit tent before going to bed and looked up at the stars which looked beautiful tonight, it gave me warm thoughts of back home, ah, the little things.

Baz's vehicle, missing fractured wheel.

What's left of a blown-up tanker.

What's left of a fuel tanker after detonating a pressure plate IED.

Blast hole from a pressure plate IED.

27/11/06

We were up for around 6.30 a.m. this morning and everyone had left the tent without warning by the time I got back from the ablutions and given no warning of what time we were going for breakfast, 'buggers'. As we were getting our kit on to leave, Shane received a phone call on the Thuraya (sat phone), ops said there would be no road moves today as there is a curfew on all traffic movement, which also gives the insurgents more time to lay IEDs.

I just relaxed most of the day although I did some press ups and dips just to keep on top of the training. As I was walking back to the tent, I bumped into Stan from the Farm (PLS Driver), I asked Stan when he'd arrived, he said he came up today. Stan said that ops forgot to tell them about the curfew and they were already on their way up, bad passage of information, Stan said, "They don't give a fuck," I said, it's just like the army we're expendable.

Well I hope we can get back tomorrow, I can't figure this team out at the moment as everyone seems to be within themselves and there is no sense of team gelling, just dry, blank and no humour. There was a loudspeaker announcement earlier from the US Army HQ cell asking for people with blood group B positive to report to the medical centre, obviously something bad had happened. The HQ cell announced later that nobody was further needed for the medical centre, so either they had enough donors or the patient had died from their wounds, I'd like to think they were OK.

One thing I've noticed about the American bases is they're like a community within a camp, they must spend millions if not billions on the infrastructure of these bases. I wish I had brought my laptop or my book to read as its times like this I think too much and get low. It's my birthday tomorrow and I know it's going to be a miserable one, no kids, or family to share it with.

I keep going through my mind how long I can keep doing this for, I so want to be back home, I'm not enjoying it as much as I used to and I want normality back in my life. It's OK saying it's for the money and trying to convince myself but is it really worth it at the end of the day? Hope we're not delayed tomorrow.

28/11/06

Happy birthday to me, well we finally left Al Asad although we got held up by a convoy, yet again, then we had to wait for the US Army EOD (Explosives Ordnance Disposal) Team to clear the Uranium route of some IEDs that had been placed there the night before. We were able to gain on time after they had been cleared although my day was dampened by Dave's driving, on the way up he nearly drove off the road and on the way down he hit a bump in the road at about 80mph. As a result of this, Mick and I hit the roof of the pod and my rifle hit me in the face 'ouch' wasn't impressed so I let him know my angry thoughts over the radio the silly sod.

We drove down without incident and were only held up once near Fallujah due to a suspect Daisy Chain IED but it was cleared after an hour. It was nice to get my kit off and get showered. I'll check the e-mails later and have a good night's sleep.

Me in the back of the pod.

Mick on the Minimi.

Baz bringing up the rear on route Uranium.

29/11/06

It was nice to get some admin done today before going out tomorrow, washed some kit and did some training. We went down to Camp Victory to collect the excursion vehicle for tomorrow's journey down south to Talil. We'll be taking six clients down for the Parsons contract. It should be a quiet journey and not as hectic as our northern trips but we'll still need to be careful of the odd IED or two.

Got paid today, which is a good thing so the bills back home can be paid, I also spoke to my mother today and the news wasn't so good as the doctor has found another lump in her breast so they'll need to do some test to make sure it's not cancerous. She' just got over one lot of chemo so I'm hoping she'll have the all clear, she's an amazing person and has been so strong through the years for me and my sisters she's wonderful.

I'll check my e-mails then it's off to bed for an early start tomorrow, I'll have to give the vehicle a quick check over in the morning as it's my turn to drive tomorrow.

30/11/06

Well it was a pleasant drive down to Talil and there weren't any problems, only some warning shots fired by the rear gunner, Rob, as a car wouldn't stay out of the hundred metre zone. We arrived at Talil just after lunch and picked up twelve Parson's clients instead of six, we then head back to camp Victory. It was noticeable that people weren't as hostile down south as they are up north which was a pleasant change.

There were a lot of Cochise travellers herding sheep and camels, I also noticed people farming salt in ponds, they would collect the salt on the surface and put it into small mounds for bagging.

I found out that Team 47 had an interesting journey back from Al Asad, as they were escorting a convoy south, passing Falujah, the first armoured vehicle was remote IEDd. Bob noticed a car and occupants acting suspiciously and told Nick who was on the Minimi to watch the vehicle, at this point the IED went off, missing the front vehicle. Nick and Dan (other top gunners) immediately opened fire on the car, John who was in another vehicle also opened fire with his M4 from the pod hatch as it drove off in the opposite direction. Conrad's Minimi wasn't fired, this was to no fault of his own as he let Ian have a go on the gun prior to the contact, I thought Ian being an ex-sergeant major from an Argyle Infantry Regiment would know better to have the safety catch off to fire the weapon but this shows his inexperience under contact and usage of weapons. I bet he got a good grilling when the guys got back and there is only so many fuck-ups thy will take, as mistakes out here costs lives.

They said they managed to get around ninety rounds off with over thirty hits on the car. Bob said the car was fish tailing everywhere so it's likely there were some direct hits on the occupants. We'll have to wait to see if there is any return info on the incident; Bob said the vehicle was clearly identified as the trigger car.

I was told by John, that while his team were at Camp Al Asad, he'd heard some shocking news that not many people knew and some were trying to keep quiet. An American security team called EODT based at Al Asad had captured ten suspected insurgents, after they had questioned them, they then blindfolded them and drove them to an isolated area where they were executed (shot in the head). If this is true then I wouldn't like to be in their shoes, places like this can make men do silly things and some bad things as their thoughts aren't straight but it doesn't give them the right to kill in cold blood even if their enemy does.

We've got tomorrow off, so will have an admin day and try and get some shopping from the green zone.

The Exertion vehicle in between the two front (out of picture) and two rear armoured PSD vehicles.

Iraqi woman farming salt near the south Tampa route to Talil.

01/12/06

Yippee, on leave next month, just thought I'd mention it not that it makes me feel good but it makes leave sound closer. Had a pretty mellow day today, we went round to the green zone to get some things from the PX but it was closed due to communication problems, 'chuckle, chuckle'. We stopped at the 5.11 shop and I bought two blue collared T-shirts as I'll be waiting for ever for them to come into the Armor stores, I couldn't help but notice all the lovely beer and lager in the shop but as this is a dry contract it's not worth losing your job over.

I spoke to John from Team 47 and he said the team was going up to Camp Spiker tomorrow, which is up the north Tampa route, he said the intelligence report from ops said there was an incident every twenty minutes on Tampa today. Well it looks like they'll be in for a busy day I just hope things go smoothly as they're escorting a large convoy tomorrow which means they'll be a large target.

I did some training this afternoon then got back to prepare food for me and Dan, poor lad couldn't buy any food today as the PX was closed so I treated him to mashed potatoes, green beans and lasagne, went down a treat. Going to check my e-mails later then have a lovely cup of cha then watch a film.

02/12/06

Team 47 left the Villa nice and early I think it was around 5am, they should have made good time up the north Tampa route to Camp Spiker. There was no electricity when the guys got up as the generator fuse had gone and the Iraqi caretaker couldn't find the keys to the other generator, so the guys had to get their head torches on to get dressed and sort their kit out.

We managed to get into the PX today so most of the team were able to get what they needed, toiletries and food, I managed not to get a Burger King or Pizza Hut as the temptation is always there to indulge in fast food while at the PX. Did some training with Mick this afternoon, then came back to a well-prepared mince and onion dinner Neil and Nick had cooked.

Shane has said our next job will probably be on the 5th December now so we'll be sitting tight, although it's better to get out as its passes time a lot quicker, one day admin, one day out is a good routine. Saturday night in Iraq, so no going down town, may have a few sneaky whiskey and cokes later, mmmm.

03/12/06

Well I was woken up by Paul early this morning as we had a power surge last night and extension leads and sockets caught fire, good old Iraqi electrical wiring nearly as bad as the Afghans'. The electrician from the MT came and managed to sort the problem out but our washing machines and microwave ovens seem to have been affected.

Team 47 haven't returned, so it looks like they will return from Camp Spiker tomorrow, we will be going to Camp Victory in the morning in order to pick Jim up from the Farm. We all had a quiet Sunday today and just relaxed. I haven't checked the news as it's nice not knowing what's happening outside the Villas in downtown Baghdad.

I cooked a lovely spaghetti bolognaise for our evening meal followed by rice pudding made by Cameron, it was a nice treat to have rice pudding and it made it feel like a real Sunday.

I've noticed the guys have opened up a lot more to me now and they seem like a genuinely good bunch of lads and more mature and varied experienced than Team 47 but that's the way it is, they've got to know you're OK as well and that you can be relied on as teams are close knit, lives depend on one another's actions and abilities.

04/12/06

We only had a local job down to Camp Victory to collect Jim as he had to pay all the teams their monthly per diem. We also had to recover a vehicle from another team that had sustained some IED damage. When we arrived back in the Villas, two Blackwater (American Security Company) Scorpion helicopters flew over, they're small but fast and aren't armed. I always see the odd one or two security guys sitting on the side trying to look cool and as if they're something out of a Hollywood film, easy target more like it and it wasn't so cool when one of their guys fell out a couple of weeks ago not sure if he lived or not.

Team 47 got in today and had a quieter time than usual, although John's vehicle got IEDd, there was no major damage and everyone was OK. Team 47 have been the most hit team so far but I hope it eases up a little as I don't want their luck to run out. We are off on a long day out tomorrow, going to ASP 7, ASP 8 and then Camp Scania. We'll be taking nine expat clients from Parson's 5.

Watched a complete series of *Shameless* tonight with the lads it was great to watch a UK comedy and have a good laugh, it's unbelievable how good it can make you feel. Well hope it's a quiet day tomorrow as I'll be commanding the second vehicle so it would be nice for it to go without incident but we'll have to see.

05/12/06

We got off nice and early today; we got to camp Falcon at around eight a.m. to collect nine Parson's 5, EOD guys (Explosives and Ordinance Demolitions) and then made our way down south to ASB 7. It was a quiet journey, fast but without incident, although we came into a serious RTA, a car had a collision with another vehicle and there were three people injured — two seriously. We couldn't stop and help as it would put us and our clients in danger although they would have been lucky to get an ambulance and Iraqi people aren't too au fait with first aid.

We got to ASB 7 in good time and dropped seven of the EOD guys off then, headed for ASB 8 which was near Zubayd. When we arrived, it was apparent that the area must have been used by the Iraqi army during the war. There was a lot of unexploded ordinance lying around and some of the bunkers showed signs of direct missile hits from the American bombardment, one in particular looked as if a giant had sat on it and left a mould of his bum.

After we dropped off our remaining two clients at ASB 8, we then travelled down to Camp Scania so we could refuel our vehicles, on the way we passed what was left of an Erinys vehicle (British Security Company) in which four people had been killed after being hit by an EFP. EFPs are one of the worst bombs, as their force just rips through armoured vehicles, not nice.

After we re-fuelled, we headed north up the Grey route back to Baghdad to Camp Falcon, to collect two EOD guys who had to be taken to Camp Victory. I'm surprised we made good time after being stuck behind a US military convoy, it's wait, or be shot by them, we have a short run up to Camp Wolf tomorrow and into Camp Victory, so we should have an early finish if all goes well.

One of the Iraqi bunkers which had been hit by an US missile during the Gulf War, it looks as if it's been sat on.

06/12/06

It was a longer day than expected today, we were meant to collect five Parson's 5 clients from Camp Falcon then take them to Camp Victory then make our way back to the Villas. Instead, we made two trips to Camp Falcon and Camp Victory then did one final journey from Camp Victory to the Villas as we had to escort an articulated lorry carrying an Iso container.

There wasn't much trouble for us today but we could see three or four fresh IED craters on our route to camp Falcon which is only twenty minutes' drive from the Villas. When we first arrived at Camp Falcon we passed a US patrol in Humvees as they were leaving, as they got to the main road, where we exited, they were attacked by small arms fire but it didn't last too long as the American's soon opened up with their 50mm gun.

We called in at an Iraqi shop at the hotel on Camp Victory, it sells all sorts of things from pirate DVDs, combat clothing, electrical equipment, cigarettes, alcohol and lots of other things. I was a bit disappointed as they tried to scam me out of $76 which wasn't very nice, I must look an easy touch or something but he was soon disappointed when I told him about his error. They billed me three times for the one day sack I bought; Iraqi's are the same as Afghan's in that sense as they'll do anything to make a quick buck.

On our return to the Villas I could hear Baz say there was a shot fired then, Rob, our rear gunner, spoke over the net he said, "Ye a sniper just took a shot at me, I wish they'd show themselves so we could play." I think the sniper would lose against the Minimi machine gun. It would have made good filming to see our team negotiate the low level electric cables as we lead the lorry back to the Villas, Cammy was on top of the container pushing the cables up over the top while Mick was guiding the driver from the front. I was concerned that Cammy was an easy target for a sniper but there was no alternative than to lift them over or rip them all down.

The driver did well to drive the lorry around the small winding streets and into the Villa's compound. We're escorting a convoy of PLS vehicles carrying explosives down south to ASP 8 tomorrow so we'll probably meet the PLS vehicles at Camp Victory on route.

07/12/06

It was an excellent day as far as having no trouble goes but the weather took a turn for the worse as it rained and was extremely cold. We met Ian and Garry at camp Victory they would be carrying explosives on the PLS vehicles for the Parsons EOD team down at ASP 8. We did a steady 80 kms an hour most of the way which is a bit nerve wracking as the slower you go the easier a target you become for an IED.

We got to ASP 8 around 10.15 a.m. and got the PLS vehicles to off-load pretty quick, the explosives will be used for controlled explosions to get rid of unexploded ordinance (bombs, missiles) that had been collected from around the area. Most of the ordinance was what the Iraqi army had left behind when they fled the area during the Gulf War. Due to the rain the mud had become like putty and Nick became a victim as he got his F350 stuck, we got one of the PLS vehicles to pull him out so it didn't put too much time on us.

After the PLS vehicles unloaded, we made our way back up north, first refuelling at Camp Scania then straight up to Camp Victory where Ian and Gary would be leaving the PSD escort team. After we had dropped Ian and Garry off at the Farm, we went to the US Army cookhouse, we were told that an hour earlier, four rockets or mortars had landed in the car park there injuring four soldiers.

Most of team 46 are in good spirits at the moment as they're going on leave on the 12th December and will be back home for Christmas, so no wonder they're all happy, the jammy buggers, no turkey for me.

Hopefully we've got the day off so I'll be able to get some admin done and sort out the vehicle as the back could do with a brush out.

ASP 8 in the middle of nowhere.

Unexploded ordinance collected and boxed ready for destruction.

PLS vehicle unloading explosives.

Nick's F350 being pulled out by PLS vehicle.

08/12/06

Today was the handover for the guys just returning from leave, the new TL (Les) took over from Shane and the other guys were told what vehicles they'd be in. I was a bit pissed off today as just when you think things are going OK, something fucks your day up. I was told I'd be in the rear vehicle with Baz, so I decided to get the back of the vehicle sorted as kit was all over the place and the spare wheel wasn't secure.

I strapped the spare wheel to the front end of the pod and put all the ammunition and flares on the right hand side so it could be got to easier and made sure the back of the vehicle was clear. My aim was to ensure everything was secure at the back of the pod so if the driver had to brake suddenly, or we crashed, things wouldn't be flying around and hit someone in the head plus the fact we'd need all the space at the back to cross deck people if their vehicle was immobilised.

I got back to our villa after sorting the kit out to be told I'd be rotating with the driver and being in the pod as cover gunner, the guy coming in from leave (Paul) would be staying on the Minimi. What's the point of rotating the positions if you're not going to do it properly just because some idiot wants to have fun on the gun, fuck we are all trained to use the Minimi so why the fuck is someone doing their own thing he must be in the 'clique'.

Oh well let him double his chances at being taken out by a sniper, Shane knows I was pissed off by this and Les, as I said, "What's the point of me sweating over arranging the back of the pod for me to do rear gunner or share the responsibility if I'm not doing it at all, I'd rather resign." Shane told Mick that if that's my attitude I'll walk him over to the admin office, oh fuck off

Shane you silly bastard, maybe if he informed me and the rest of the guys what the fuck is going on in the team it wouldn't be such a guessing game.

Sometimes I think if it wasn't for the money and the buzz, I'd be out of here in a flash; it's a shame you just have to put up with the same shit different place, same fucking idiots who think they know it all but need a good reality slap in the face or punch. It's hard sometimes to hold it in and not just scream in their faces and say, "Just shut the fuck up, and just do the job you're paid for and inform the guys on what your plans are instead of fucking everyone around." Anyway, sorry about the moan as it's the only place that's safe to have a good angry outburst without someone passing what you've said on to someone else.

We got information that one of the Armor Group call signs was ambushed up near Mosul today and they lost one of their vehicles, we didn't get any news on how many casualties there were so we'll just have to wait and see what the intelligence report says tomorrow.

09/12/06

Bob and I were looking at the attack scale in Baghdad and north Iraq yesterday and found there had been over one hundred and forty attacks on coalition Fforces, Iraqi army and private security companies (in one day). The most significant attack was on US Army Abraham tank that was destroyed by a large IED which left a seventeen by twenty feet crater, the insurgents are starting to use pressure plate IEDs on speed bumps now which have been quite effective.

This evening, we all had a bit of a scare as we heard automatic gunfire outside our villa and presumed we were under attack as we thought the guards were opening up on insurgents attacking our compound. There were tracer rounds lighting up the sky and bullets landing all around us like raindrops, I asked the guard if he would need us to get our weapons and he said, "Oh, no, we are celebrating Iraq beating Uzbekistan in football." Can you believe it.

It's been a day of surprises today as we've been told we'll be losing days off our leave and that it will be more of a nine weeks on and three weeks on leave instead of eight and four. The guys weren't impressed but like I tried to tell the new guys it's the same in other companies, things don't run as they're meant to but it would be nice to have it in our contract. To add salt to the wound, they've decided to turn our internet off as they say someone has been tampering with the wiring. I don't think anyone would have the guts due to the risk of being electrocuted. There's one quote John said to me that is so true, 'we are lions being led by donkeys'.

Team 47 did some training today as they got Chris back as TL; he was in the Royal Welch Fusiliers while I was there in Berlin. Chris is your typical keen, 'I wish I didn't leave the Army', type of guy and may cause some friction with the older lads. John is already showing signs of being fed up with the crap factor and as he's old school 2 Para from when paratroopers were still jumping out of a balloon on Queens Avenue in Aldershot, I can't blame him being airborne trained myself, we will always be treated like mercenaries out here — used and expendable.

I've enjoyed my talks with Bob as he is ex RUC (Royal Ulster Constabulary) but since the ceasefire in Ireland, it has been renamed, we've been talking about areas we are both familiar with. Bob said he'd worked in Belfast near Woodbourne RUC station where I was based while serving in the forces during my tour in Northern Ireland in 1992, it's hard to forget the Twinbrooks, Poleglass estate, Falls Road and the Mill.

Well, hopefully, we'll all be in a better mood tomorrow as we've been static for a couple of days due to the change-over and people get bored easily out here if they're not busy.

10/12/06

It's just been a watching a DVD type of day today although it is Sunday so it was nice to relax, I did do some training this afternoon though. The guys are still pissed off about our internet being switched off as it feels like some sort of punishment for no reason, there will be mutiny before long. It looks like we'll be going out on our next job on the 14th December, so another few days off by the look of things. It'll be nice to get out as I'm so bored with just sitting around the Villa and you soon miss the rush of being out in the thick of it.

Team 47 are off to Camp Buckmaster in the next two days so they'll be out before my team, more than likely they'll run into some trouble as they're going up north. I feel there is still a bit of tension in the air at the moment, as the Villa isn't exactly the most comfortable of accommodations and beside the faulty wiring and the shortage of hot water, overcrowding and most of all, no communications, as we've no internet tempers will fray. I hope things improve, otherwise it's going to be a miserable

Christmas even if Santa does risk coming to Iraq to drop our presents off.

11/12/06

Yippee, the internet is back on; all they need to do now is fix our Sky system as well, enough whinging for now as it won't help repair anything. Half of our team go on leave tomorrow, the jammy buggers, and they'll get Christmas and New Year back home but they deserve it.

Team 47 are off on a job tomorrow so they will be gone for a day or two I just hope they have a safe ride up north as things are still pretty bad on the north Tampa run. A low-profile PSD security person was kidnapped today at an insurgent checkpoint where they were probably dressed as IP's (Iraqi Police). It still looks as if we won't be out on a job until the 14th December so we're just preparing kit at the moment and giving the vehicles a good going over.

Had a sneaky drink of JD and Coke with Bob, Mick and John tonight, reminiscing over the days when we were still in the army. We were talking about our airborne days in Aldershot and where some of our friends are now with the likes of Graham Hill who was on selection with me. Graham is probably still in Hereford loving the green machine as usual, although I'll never forget his first job for the SAS didn't go as planned when they rescued the Royal Irish Regiment personnel in Sierra Leone.

Poor old Graham got some friendly mortar shrapnel in the leg as they entered the Gorillas' camp, 2 Para were laying mortars down while the twenty-two lads were descending on rope from the helicopters but the shrapnel was cutting through the mud huts as if it was butter. Unfortunately, Graham's team lost one of their guys as he was shot as he was descending the rope.

I bet it's crazy back home at the moment with all the Christmas shopping and busy streets in Swansea and all the shopping rage but that's one thing I won't miss. At least I'll miss the Christmas panic shopping but I'll probably catch the January sales.

12/12/06

I watched a Syrian TV channel this morning while having some breakfast and couldn't believe the propaganda it was showing, it was like an insurgent recruiting video (Al-Rashedeen Army). It firstly showed wounded children from the Gulf War and there was no measure in how graphic the scenes were, showing dead babies and children with limbs that had been blown off. They made sure they made the American soldiers look as bad as possible and then showed insurgent footage of IEDs, mortar and sniper attacks on US military.

They also showed footage of an interview with the brigade commander of the insurgent sniper team in Baghdad. They were bragging how they had shot over six hundred American soldiers, I think there's a little exaggeration on the body count and the last I'd heard the main insurgent sniper had been captured. There's probably someone who will fill his place and I've seen the results of the snipers' work when they killed one of the Parson drivers up near Sammarra.

Our team went to the green zone today to get some more food and replacement mattresses as the ones we have got just feel like springs covered in cloth. We refuelled the vehicles ready for

Thursday so we can just go straight from camp Victory after we have collected the excursion vehicles. It was another nasty day in Baghdad today as a suicide bomber killed forty-five people, he was disguised as a person looking for workers, and he got the people to get into the minibus which he was driving then set the bomb off. There were another two bombs that exploded in the Shiite area of Baghdad so no doubt there will be revenge attacks.

Syrian TV channel showing American soldier with an injured Iraqi.

Syrian TV showing insurgent snipers shooting US soldiers.

13/12/06

Well the extra mattress I bought yesterday worked a treat and gave me a good night's sleep, got up this morning and had a lovely bottle wash which gave flashbacks of Sharan in Afghanistan, brrrrr. We'll give the vehicles a final check-over later, God knows why, as they've been done twice but I think Les wants to get peace of mind.

Team 47 came back without incident today so no news is good news. Unfortunately, Armor lost two people today, one expat and one national. They were killed by an EFP (Explosive Formed Projectile) in southern Iraq near Kirkush, the expat was the vehicle commander and the national was driving. We'll probably get more news on what happened tomorrow, we're off to ASP 7 and ASP 8 tomorrow to collect clients so I hope it's another quiet south run.

14/12/06

It was another smooth run down south to ASP 7 and ASP 8 today, the only real incident didn't involve any insurgents but I'll explain what happened later. We took two Excursion vehicles today as we had to collect nine Parson clients with luggage who were going on Christmas leave. The US military had checked the route so there was little or no chance that there would have been any IEDs on our route.

After we had left ASP 7, we followed a narrow road which ran along a river, we were just about to come to a sharp right hand turn over a narrow bridge when I saw Camy braking hard in front of me. It was Les's vehicle then John's Excursion then Camy, me and finally Baz. Camy tried braking (so he says) but didn't have enough time to stop and shunted John's Excursion vehicle. There was little damage to either vehicle which isn't a surprise as both vehicles have reinforced armour; the only damage I would think is to Camy's pride, 'dented' I'd say.

There were a lot of dead dogs on the road today which can be worrying as the insurgents have been known to stuff dead dogs with explosives in the past and detonate them when US military or security companies drive round them. I wonder how the north run went for Team 47 as there has rarely been an occasion when any team has gone up north and hasn't been attacked. Well it's an admin day tomorrow then I think we've got a job on Saturday, not to sure of where we're going yet.

15/12/06

What a morning I feel I am feeling the repercussions of David Gwillym (Kiwi), how can you trust some people. I made some late breakfast this morning and sat down to watch some TV with Camy and Dave (cockney). Someone walked past and slammed the kitchen door so me and Camy shouted simultaneously, "Slam the door, why don't you?" then the person came back to slam it again.

I got up to look in the kitchen to see who it was, it was Paul (Scottish lad) don't slam the door please, I said, "I'll slam the door if I want, you got a problem with that?" I walked away back into the TV room then Paul came in and said, "Stop your mouthing who do you think you are, you've only been here for two minutes."

"Two minutes, I said, who the fuck are you?" Anyway a lot of verbal abuse was exchanged but during it I found out that Paul had heard from Team 41 that I'd been slagging the guys off in Team 47, I informed him that I wasn't happy in the team and yes there were one or two people who I didn't see eye to eye with.

I said with me knowing Dave (Kiwi) didn't help as I've been tarred with the same brush as him and I explained that I only knew him as an acquaintance and even though he was in Afghanistan I didn't know him as an operator on the ground. I told Paul I hadn't a bad word to say about anyone in Team 46 and was glad to be working with the guys and when asked I've always said they are a good bunch of guys since I've got to know them. I also mentioned the fact that Dave (Kiwi) had used info from my CV to buff up his own CV, as for the person I am, nobody really knows me or what I've done in the army and the SF stuff I've done I am proud of.

Anyway, we had a lot of bitching but Paul kept shouting in my face so we ended up in a tussle. I think he was surprised as I fear no man and fair do's he's six feet two in height. We rolled round in the kitchen banging off the table. I fell back onto the floor and he fell on me. I grabbed his face and plunged both my thumbs into his eyes then took a firm squeeze of his testicles. At this point he tried to bite my face but as he did so I tightened my squeeze and he soon stopped.

I tried to get him to one side but it was difficult to get him over as he's a lump of a lad, then the other guys burst in the kitchen and pulled us apart. Paul was still mouthing off at me and shouting verbal abuse, so in temper, I just grabbed the nearest chair and flung it at him. I said you don't know me and have no right to judge who I am if I was you, I'd watch yourself. I took a couple of minutes to cool down as did Paul and we were both bleeding and he couldn't see out of one of his eyes.

I think Paul understood where I was coming from and I know I can sometimes have a loud sense of humour, but I have got experience out here as well as Afghanistan and although some guys have done work in Iraq longer than me, I know my job and am good at it. Paul came to see me a bit later and said shall we shake and forget it or just go on as we are? I said,

"I'll shake, but you got to know me for who I am and not what other people's opinions are."

We shook hands and Paul said, "Now we can talk, Tony?"

Les came to see me and said it would be brushed under the carpet as he didn't want either of us losing our jobs but he said he wouldn't put me and Paul in the same vehicle. I told Les it wouldn't affect me working with Paul as we're all big boys and some things needed to be aired. I'll be keeping a distance from gossiping bastards in the future and the likes of Dave Gwillym. We have our own worries out here and tension in the team is no good as we depend on one another and our lives depend on our professionalism. Noli Illegitemi Carborndum (Don't let the bastards grind you down). I always wonder was it Paul's behaviour that would cost him his life? But no man deserves to be killed the way Paul was, cowardly I'd say. Paul would later be killed by a fellow security operator while working in Camp Victory, Baghdad, rest in peace butty.

Just had our brief and we're going to ASP 8 first thing tomorrow then ASP 7, the intelligence reports say there was some small arms fire in the area and there is a lot of insurgent activity and that the Iraqi army are an unreliable source which isn't a surprise. Team 47 will probably be back tomorrow as they haven't arrived back at the Villas, I spoke to a lad who's just joined Team 47 (Gordon) and he says he isn't too keen on staying with Team 47 — that doesn't surprise me.

Gordon and I had a chat about SAS selection, he said he VW (Voluntary Withdrawal) from the jungle phase of the course, which is definitely the hardest part. Gordon said he wished he'd tried again. I told him it will eat at him the fact he hasn't had another try as I went back a second time. He could go for 21 SAS the Territorial Army way in, it'll just mean he'll be part time but still join the regular SAS on some missions.

16/12/06

We got to Camp Victory about 07.30 a.m. this morning and left with three clients at about 08.30 a.m. for ASP 8. We would be able to set off much earlier if it wasn't for the fact of collecting clients from camp Victory as it so large. After entering the main entrance, it takes us forty minutes to get to the Farm. It was going well down the usual south route until we had to stop as a US military EOD team had found an IED on our route, and by the sound of the controlled explosion, it was a big one.

We continued on our route until we arrived at Scania where we refuelled our vehicles but as we were about to leave Scania, we were told they'd found another IED one mile from the south. There was no other option but to take a detour through a red area which isn't good, so we all were on our toes. After detouring around, we got back on track and arrived at ASP 8 at around lunchtime. We were going to stay for a while to see the Parson 5 demolition team do a controlled explosion to get rid of some ammunition but as he said, "Fire in the hole." (Typical American bomb slang) there was nothing.

Typical, I was hoping to get some good footage of the explosion and it didn't go to plan, hopefully I'll be there when they're doing another big bang. Our team left ASP 8 at around 13.30 p.m. and had a smooth drive up to ASP 7 where we collected three clients to take back to Baghdad. As we were driving back, Les had a call from ops they said that the vehicle we had leant to another team had been IED twice today so it looks like it may come back with a few dents.

Things have settled now since yesterday's incident with Paul and I've noticed he's speaking a lot better to me now, I chuckled when I was speaking to Mick today as he said, "Paul was mouthing and using his size to intimidate you thinking you'd back down but I think he bit off more than he could chew." I'm just glad it was aired in the open and we got our differences sorted as we both can get on with each other now and do our jobs and he will have more respect for me now.

Mick and I discussed how Team 46 had been lucky for having such a quiet time at the moment and no contacts, IEDs etc. I said it was my father doing his guardian angel bit. I asked Mick if his parents were still alive, he said his father died when he was only seven. I couldn't have imagined not spending the later years of my life without my dad and him not seeing my children and the people in my life. Mick seemed comfortable talking about his dad; he said that his dad died in a work-related accident, he said his father was crushed by the forklift truck he was driving when it crashed.

I like Mick's company as he's a warm character and seems to have a big heart and thinks of his family a lot, he is a good operator and even though he has come from a ten-year period in the Territorial Army, he has spent a long time doing operations in Iraq. Mick's comment as we arrived back today brought a smile to my face, he said, "We've got two guardian angels not one looking after us that's why we're OK." Well I hope they don't mind doing the overtime as we need all the luck we can get out here as fate comes on swift wings.

Our vehicle's on stop waiting for the IED to be detonated so we can continue another Armor call sign to our right.

The view to the rear of our vehicles, you'd think the insurgents wouldn't be able to plant IEDs so close to a US military checkpoint (on bridge) but they are efficient at what they do.

17/12/06

It looks like all the guys in the Villa won't be getting food from the local shop anymore, we have two cleaners who are sisters, Zahra and Izrah, who usually go and get odds and ends we require if we're desperate for things. They normally go to the shop across the street and a local market nearby but today they were threatened by one of our own Iraqi guards and warned if they do it again they'll be killed.

Nick said they're trying to find out who threatened the sisters in order to sack him but that's the way this place is, you never know who you can trust. The cleaners will need to be careful from now on and the guys in the villa will have to stick with shopping at the PX only from now on.

I cooked a lovely stir fry for me, John, Bob and Nick tonight it was nice for all of us to sit down and relax having a good meal as the guys are of cut again tomorrow off up north to camp Buckmaster. Our team isn't going out until the 20th December and more than likely it'll be down south, well at least there is more chance of it being a trouble-free day.

I spoke to the kids today for the first time in four months, Charmaine sounded miserable but sounded glad to talk about Christmas presents and the play she's doing at school. Nico is still my baby and even though he's six, he sounds so grown up sometimes mind it hurt when he said, "I don't know if I love you, Dad." It felt as if a knife had been driven through my heart, but he's young and that's the price of not being there for them, I wish I could give this up tomorrow but it's do this and get my life sorted or be back home and struggle. At least life will be a lot easier after finishing this contract and I can concentrate on the kids more as I miss doing things with them.

18/12/06

It's been a quiet day today as Team 47 left nice and early around 06.00 a.m. this morning so we had the Villa to ourselves today. I had a good training session this afternoon then cooked some food, I've been getting steak from the PX and it's a really nice treat compared to tinned food all the time.

We all had our names put into a hat today for a spamming as another team was a man down, supposedly one of their guys is refusing to go out on a job tomorrow as they've been attacked every time they've done the route. Unfortunately, Dave's name was chosen to join the team so I hope things go OK and the guy who didn't go, well I hope he's on the next plane home as we all know the risks but still get on with the job.

We've got a quick PSD job tomorrow as we have got to collect nine clients from the Farm then take them to the airport.

19/12/06

I was on the Minimi today when we did the airport run, I forgot how physically fit you have to be to throw the gun around on the swing arm from left to right and covering both sides. I got a little overdressed as I thought it would be another cold day but no, I was sweating my arse off, sunny skies. We even managed to call into the hotel and pay a visit to the Iraqi shop where I and Mick picked up some festive treats.

We collected four new guys today but I'm not sure what team they'll be joining but there has been a lot of guys resigning and moving onto Aegis leaving gaps in Armor, I'm not up for doing nine weeks on and three weeks off rotation with Aegis. We're going to ASP 7 tomorrow and I'll be on top gunner on the Minimi for the third vehicle so my arms will be aching by the time I get back to the Villas.

Team 47 got back this evening, the route up to Buckmaster was a bit slow due to three IEDs and one dead body on the side of the road of someone who had been executed, at least the journey back went without incident. Both teams are going to ASP 7 tomorrow so hopefully it'll be a quiet day, we should get back before Team 47 as they're escorting convoy vehicles but we'll see.

20/12/06

Team 47 had a rough start this morning as they are the second team to lose a wheel while on a job. As they left the Villas this morning, one of their vehicle's front wheels sheared off and the vehicle was immobilised, now all the F350s have been called into the servicing bay to be checked for faults. Our team had collected our clients and started on our journey down the south Tampa route before Team 47 had got to camp Victory to meet the trucks they were escorting.

We had a clear run all the way to ASP 7 but had to wait for an hour before we could leave as one of the clients was the health and safety assessment officer, he had to complete a complete H&S check of the camp.

After Team 47 had their vehicle repaired they set off again, as they were passing the first IP (Iraqi Police) checkpoint they heard a loud explosion, it was a suicide bomber about a kilometre away. In total, eleven people were killed mostly IP, Bob said that after the explosion some IP vehicles came past with injured and dead from the blast, Bob said he could see a young IP officer crying frantically over the body of one of the dead IP officers who was probably a relative.

Even though our team had an incident free run down south, Team 47 weren't so lucky and got IED on their way, fortunately no one was hurt but one of the vehicles took a little shrapnel. Team 47 were delivering an Eagle Eye Surveillance System to ASP 7 worth over three million pounds, but as it can see up to twelve kilometres away, I suppose it has its advantages.

Both teams got back to Baghdad without anything happening although when we were approaching the Tampa entrance I could see a crowd of people near the river and as I was top gunner I had a clear view of what was going on. I noticed there was a dead body floating face down in the river, unbelievably it's quite a common thing in Iraq and it would be surprising how many bodies would turn up if you were to run a net across the rivers.

Well no news of any jobs at the moment but hopefully we'll be sat tight until after Christmas, the guys are still working on how we can throw a Christmas meal together but I think there's little hope.

Guys from my vehicle Ray (Ex RUC) and John (Ex PWRR).

Our team being briefed on the IED incident by members of Team 47, at the front of Les's vehicle you can see the EFP countermeasure bar which is in its lowered position.

IED shrapnel impact on the driver's side of one of Team 47 vehicles which was caught by the IED blast.

Me on the Minimi (Gunner).

21/12/06

It's been *Changing Rooms* this morning as all of Team 47 has been moving upstairs and all of Team 46 has moved downstairs. This has all been because someone has been complaining but won't admit to doing so (spineless bastard). We are living in a close environment, in accommodation which should be condemned, with a multitude of personalities not to mention the tension of doing the job, so tempers will boil. We go on leave in three weeks, so beds will become available and all this moving will be in vain as the guys coming back in will just jump into any bed space.

My team were given a fast ball to the airport today we were given fifteen minutes to get our kit on, as I went to collect the

Minimi it had already been taken by Dave. I ask Les if it would be all right to stay as I would be the floating bloke and as we were only taking three vehicles there would be little point in going and if truth be known I wanted to be able to phone my mother to find out how her hospital appointment went today.

Well, everyone has done the move and as I predicted there is a lot of tension among the guys, all my room mates John, Bob and Nick have moved upstairs. Two guys from my team have moved in Marcus (ex PWOR, Prince of Wales Own Regiment) and John (ex Argyles), Marcus is a bit difficult to work out as he only speaks now and then and likes his own space. John is a little chattier but seems a bit low today as the move has stressed him out; I've already given John the gypsies warning about no smoking in the room as I can't stand selfish smokers who don't care where they light up.

We haven't got any tasks until Christmas Eve as far as we know at the moment but we will probably get a fast ball or two before then.

22/12/06

Another lazy day today, although I did my usual gym visit. I took the gas bottles over to the Iraqi guards to make sure we can cook our Christmas dinner and hopefully the gas bottles will come back with gas inside not explosives. Team 47 are going down to Hila on Christmas Eve, they'll be doing a range day and then having their Christmas day dinner there which is good as we'll have more room in our villa.

I think some of the guys are feeling the Christmas blues as there are a few faces dragging on the floor but I can sympathise with them, I've been lucky as this is the only Christmas I've spent away from home even including the sixteen years I did in the army. It seems unbelievable that for some lads this will be their fourth consecutive Christmas away.

I think Conrad is feeling it a bit as he has lots to sort out back home, with sorting out his new mortgage and the fact that his vehicle was IEDd on the way to ASP 7 the other day doesn't help. Conrad's ears were ringing for a couple of hours after and brought reality right to his door, at least he's OK I would like to think he'll stay though as it would be a shame to see him make the decision to leave.

23/12/06

Got our Christmas food shopping in today which will be a chicken dinner instead of turkey but as long as there's gravy I'll be happy. I spoke with John today and he's not happy with going to Hila, one reason is because there will be little traffic which makes them an easy target and the other is the fact that Chris (TL) is trying to run it like a military school. Chris wants the vehicle commanders to do "Gun Parade" (going around giving the lads brandy in tea first thing in the morning) on Christmas morning and for them to cook Christmas dinner as well, embarrassing I'd say.

I feel that's why there is such a divide in Team 47, as Chris causes so much animosity amongst the guys it becomes unbearable. Marcus and I walked into the kitchen tonight to make a cup of tea only to walk into Chris and Nick arguing. Chris has said to his team basically, that if they're suspicious of anyone they should shoot them. Nick rightly disagrees with this as you need to be certain before you take the shot and this isn't Iraq three years ago where you could have got away with it. This is here and now and if you kill an innocent person you will go to jail, you can't afford to make mistakes and you need to be one hundred per cent sure before you pull that trigger and if you can't make that decision you shouldn't be out here.

Well, I hope Team 47 have a good Christmas in Hila, that is if they go, that's if the crappie weather stays as it did today, rain, then they'll have no top cover (helicopters) so they stay put in the Villa's.

24/12/06

Well it's Christmas Eve and we have got our treats sorted for tomorrow thanks to the guys going into the green zone to do some last-minute shopping, we'll have a nice dinner, pudding for after, crate of beer and snacks. Team 47 left for Hila early this morning so hopefully they had a quiet run down, unfortunately one of the PWC convoy teams was hit today by an IED, two Iraqi nationals were killed and one New Zealand expat Armour guy was injured.

I hope there aren't any more incidents now as it would be nice to have a quiet Christmas but as the saying goes there is no rest for the wicked and there's plenty of them out here. I did my last training session before taking a two day break, while I was on my way back from the gym I could see a number of people gathered together and it seemed as if there was a commotion. As I approached, it became apparent what was going on, it was the father of one of the Iraqi nationals working for Armor who was killed today. His brother was also there as he was doing guard duty in the Villas, I could see the pain in the father's eyes and could only imagine the pain he must have been feeling.

I asked what was going on and I was told in broken English, "The father, his son killed in explosion." The father cried and kept wailing in Arabic, he was so distraught with anger and grief. I felt useless in knowing how to console him and said to one of the guards I was sorry for his loss and shook the guard's hand.

As I walked away I felt unbelievably sad at how this could happen on Christmas Eve of all days, where is the peace in violence and how does it stop, never I'd say.

25/12/06

It was a great day today, Baz and Chris did an excellent job on the dinner and Cammy did a Christmas pudding with cream and custard. All the guys chipped in today and helped in some way to sort out getting the Christmas dinner ready. It was strange being away from home for Christmas Day and here we are blind to all the manic festive celebrations going on back home, a phone call to all the family reminded me of what I was missing.

I got a text from Conrad (Team 47) and he said they had a good Christmas Eve except for the fourteen mortars they had fired at the camp in Hila. I told Conrad he was lucky as at least he had fireworks, he did see the funny side, fair dos. We all relaxed in the TV room after food and had a few sociable drinks and watched a classic film we all like *Zulu* which makes the guys laugh at the Welsh guys in the film on about their choir singing.

We had a bit of a surprise which spoilt the mood; we were told by Les that some of the Fijians have resigned so our team will have to stand in for them on a convoy task up north. The problem being is that this duty isn't in our contract so how does it affect our life insurance, and the rest of the team aren't happy but same shit different company, just got to get on with it and bite the bullet, literally.

We're going to Al Asad up north so we should be in for some fun and it definitely won't be as peaceful as our south runs, so ready to go for 5:30am hopefully all will go OK.

Team 46 ready to tuck into their Christmas dinner.

A Christmas afternoon in front of the TV letting the food settle while watching the film Zulu

26/12/06

The morning started as the day would go on this morning, we found out that the Fijians had resigned as they didn't want to do top caver and wanted to drive as another two of their guys got injured in an IED blast. We were delayed leaving with Team 44 as there was a lot of in-house politics and nothing was getting solved, and to add to problems, one of the vehicles got a puncture before we had got anywhere.

It was an unusually quiet run up to Al Asad and we didn't come into any contacts on route although we did drive past an IED but it didn't go off. The vehicle problems were a nightmare and it was another slow boring IED, hole dodging trip along Uranium. One of the convoy trucks broke down on the way and after they had put another truck on the trailer it was pulling, I notice the trailer was too close to the back of the truck.

This caused the truck's wheel guards to wedge against the trailer, luckily an American female officer came to our rescue. Lauran was fortunately a captain in the Mechanical Engineers Corps and she got one of her female mechanical engineers to go to work on the vehicle straight away. It took about forty minutes for the problem to be solved then we carried on to Al Asad, we got the vehicles to the Parsons' vehicle yard where they'll stay overnight ready for tomorrows move to their final drop off point.

On my way up, I shared my vehicle with Dave Potter (ex 1 Para) he, like others, has grown tired of the bad admin within the company and is tempted to look for a different contract. Dave said he is also getting married and doesn't want to be doing this work for too long which is understandable.

I talked to Dave about when my father died last year, as in the morning while refuelling our vehicle in camp Victory I had seen a big JCB, this gave me a flashback to seeing my father behind the controls of a digger. I talked about how I felt, the loss, how much I missed him and how you should say whatever you're feeling at the time you want to say it as it's too late to tell someone how much you love them when they are dead.

Dave said he had lost a friend out in Iraq recently, David Vine it was, then I realised who he was, he was one of the five people killed when a truck hit their armoured vehicle head on. Dave said David was only twenty-seven when he was killed and that he attended his funeral, he said his parent asked him how he actually died but Dave really couldn't go into graphic detail. David's parents wouldn't have liked to hear that he was crushed beyond belief with his head cracked open. It's best to keep those memories deep away in the dark of your mind.

Hopefully we'll be back in Baghdad tomorrow night but we'll see how the drop off goes and how quick they unload the vehicles.

One of many hold-ups on the dreaded Uranium Road.

US Army cruising by as we are held up by another vehicle problem.

The truck guard wedged on the trailer.

Female mechanic working on the trailer.

Lauran in the middle of the picture checking her soldiers work.

27/12/06

We all had a pretty good sleep in the heated tents at the Parson's yard at Al Asad; I got up nice and early so I could get a good breakfast as I knew we'd be on the road all day. We escorted a convoy of ten vehicles up to the new location 'Camp Duhlab' which is only about thirty minutes away from Al Asad but it is in a pretty dangerous area on the Bronze route which is code black (Extremely Dangerous).

There will be a Parson's 5 EOD team at camp Duhlab, it was once an Iraqi ammunition depot and the area is scattered with ordnance so it will need to be disposed of. The Parson's team will need to set up a base camp there prior to starting work and most of the move was done today, they will require accommodation, shower/ablutions block, canteen and stores etc.

After our trucks had off-loaded we made our way back down route Uranium or as I've come to know it as the bumpy holy road. Our return drive was much faster than on the way up but we didn't know what we were about to drive into after passing Fallujah. We were approaching Abu Ghraib at around 4pm and dusk was setting, the sun looked beautiful as it was lowering in the sky. I was driving the rear vehicle with Dave as commander; we were keeping the convoy together and making sure there were no gaps.

As we were approaching Abu Ghraib, where there are fields and small wooded areas, I noticed a US armoured call sign approaching on the other side of the motorway then all of a sudden there was an enormous blast to our right. Luckily the insurgents had set the IED off early and the blast went in between the vehicles, contact was given over the radio and we kept on driving. As we continued, immediately. David and I heard Mike in the front vehicle shout over the radio, "We're taking fire from the right." At this point David and I noticed tracer bullets flying past the vehicles in front of us in a glowing rain of red and orange with the occasional round ricocheting off the motorway barriers.

I looked on as we were engulfed by the gun fire, our Fijian top cover opened fire on the insurgent position as it was given away with the tracer rounds, they were firing at us. There were continuous cracks of bullets flying over the top of our vehicle, as we were passing the contact point, I could see the tracer bullets shoot over the top of our vehicle whistling past our Fijian top cover's head. I was surprised none of the trucks were hit or that any of the drivers panicked and stopped, as if this had happened, we would have had no other choice but to stop and fight as we wouldn't be able to leave a truck and driver behind.

As we continued down the road, I noticed that the steering on my vehicle was starting to vibrate, I asked Dave to take a look in the mirror and see if we had a puncture from the contact. One of our right-hand tyres had been shot and was losing air but luckily, we were running on run flats so we were able to travel a little distance before changing the tyre. We came up to a bridge on the far side of Abu Ghraib where I thought it would be safe to change the tyre, we could go under the bridge and use it as cover and the trucks would cover us from either side as well. Dave had other plans and wanted to do it in the open but as he was making a fuss about stopping prior to the bridge I did so.

Next time I'll go with my own instincts and do it the safe way but at least we all made it back in safe and sound. After dropping the trucks of at Camp Victory we returned to the Villas for a welcoming hot shower. Off to ASP 7 and ASP 8 tomorrow so hopefully a quiet day.

Our tent accommodation, very comfortable under the circumstances.

Getting ready to bring the vehicles into Camp Duhlab.

A JCB clears ordnance that may be on the surface in order to put the trailers and loads down.

Trailers being dropped carrying the ablutions, and accommodation.

An ING lookout point on the hill in the distance, camp Duhlab is in a quite a remote area and insurgents are known to be active in the area.

28/12/06

It was our usual quiet run down south today and went for the different option of going to ASP 8 first then to ASP 7. We took four clients down and brought four clients back to Camp Victory, I suppose we made good time due to the smooth run and there was little traffic to hold us up not even too many US military call signs. We refuelled at Camp Scania and set off for ASP 8 before 10.30 a.m.

We had a bit of a drama getting into camp Victory in the morning as we all need to be issued our MNFI identity cards and as we haven't been issued them yet we had to hand our passports in to the US Military ID office where we encountered a grumpy US military sergeant who was probably fed up with getting stick off private security guys who get paid more than him.

We have got tomorrow off so I'll be able to get some washing done and have a good training session and hopefully we'll be going up north on our next task but who knows.

Just about to arrive at Camp Scania to refuel before setting of for ASP 8, clear roads.

Controlled explosion at ASP 8 carried in order to destroy unexploded ordnance.

29/12/06

We heard this morning, that Team 47 will be disbanded in two weeks due to Parson 5 cut backs, I'm just hoping that it won't affect our team as I'll be gutted if I have to find work again and start chasing companies up in UK and go through the interview thing. Some of the lads in Team 47 are absolutely gutted especially the one or two who have just bought their own place.

It's a case of just hoping you get moved onto another contract or you find something in the New Year, it gets a bit stale towards the end of the financial year and the companies rarely recruit during that time. Well, all I can do is hope and pray that I'll be OK and I can still look forward to wages going into my bank. It has been confirmed now and Chris Agey (Project Manager) has briefed the TLs on what's happening with the teams.

Team 47 will definitely be disbanded although some of the guys will be put onto other contracts like PWC Agility and Afghanistan. The guys that are on leave will not be returning but they will be put onto new contracts when they become available, unfortunately Sam (Scouse) and Paul from our team have been laid off as well.

This is a result of Parson 5 cutting back on expenditure and as a result, like any company, job cuts will happen, I just hope our Team will be left alone now. As a result of Team 47 disbanding our team will now also carry out convoy work as well as PSD jobs, so we'll be getting contacts more regular but at least we're still here. We haven't been told when our next job is but it won't be long and we should be doing more runs up north as well.

The only other thing is Saddam Hussein may be getting executed tomorrow for his crimes against humanity, if he is killed, I think there will be a lot of trouble over the next few weeks but we'll just have to wait and see.

30/12/06

Saddam Hussein was executed this morning at Camp Justice in the district of Kamhadiyah just before six a.m., I think he deserved to be punished for the crimes he committed but was it necessary to kill him and will anything be gained by his death or will he become a martyr. His death can be justified for the massacre of the Kurds, north Iraq, where he gassed hundreds including women and children, did those things go through his mind before the noose tightened around his neck.

We still have no news about any jobs that may be coming up and I'm sure after Saddam Hussein's execution there will be little road movement. There have been a lot of car bombs in Baghdad today, one killing over thirty-five people but the worst is yet to come I would think. I'd like to get out now as staying in the Villa just gets a little cramped after a while and boredom sets in pretty quickly.

Had a good chat with Mick tonight and a couple of sociable drinks, Mick said he will be going on compassionate leave prior to us leaving on the 12th January as his grandfather passed away last night. I give my condolences to him but Mick seemed quite emotional and he was overcome with the thoughts of his father's death. He said his grandfather would be buried in the same grave as his father and that it would bring upsetting memories back for his mum.

I talked to Baz, Lee and Mick how difficult I found it to do the speech at my father's funeral, but life goes on and I know he will be at peace now. Mick was quite tearful so I gave him a manly shoulder rub and put my arm around his shoulder and told him things would be OK. Mick misses the time he could have spent with his father and its plain to see but he deals with it well, the hurt will always be there.

Saddam Hussein just before his execution.

31/12/06

New Year's Eve 2006 and we are soon to bring in 2007, what will it bring? Sadness, happiness, death, new life, peace and forgiveness but who knows we will only know when it happens. I phoned my mum and got some bad news about an old school friend, David Miller. Unfortunately, his wife lost her battle with cancer and died in the last few days at the young age of thirty-three.

David and I were close friends in Maesyrdderwen comprehensive school, we were both keen rugby players and both played for the Swansea Valley school boys' team and we both made the Welsh Junior Fly-Fishing Team in Llandegfed.

My thoughts go out to David and his four-year-old daughter. David is a lovely person and we only spoke recently when I was home last, I can't imagine the emotions he must be feeling at the moment. I will definitely call in to see him when I get back as I think he is going to need a lot of support although his mum, dad and sister are great, they'll give him plenty of support.

Finish 2006 off with one or two quiet drinks and then a DVD before bed and in the morning it'll be 2007, may the New Year be good, happy and prosperous. I give some chocolates and sweets to the children who live in the Iraqi villas next to ours today, they were really excited but it made me feel good as it's what Christmas is about, giving.

01/01/07

It was a quiet New Year's Day today and we all just chilled out in our own way, I'm starting to look forward to getting home for some time off now as its well deserved. Our team is going up north tomorrow, we'll be going to Camp Wolf then onto Al Asad and the next day we're going to Camp Duhlab then back to Camp Victory.

I've got a feeling we'll definitely be running into trouble on route but whether it on our way or on the way back we will just have to wait and see. Well, Team 47 won't be doing any more tasks now as their team has disbanded, some guys are waiting to move on to PWC contract while the rest wait to return to the UK on the 9th January.

02/01/07

To my surprise, we had a pleasant drive up to Al Asad and we didn't even have any problems coming through Abu Ghraib which is good in the long run but as we were doing a PSD run and not a convoy, we had speed on our side. As we were passing the place where we were attacked before I noticed a US military call sign spraying petrol on the long reeds and grass to burn them.

They're probably burning the reeds and grass to prevent the insurgents from having cover and so the military have better vision of where to shoot. We didn't end up going to camp Wolf so we had an early finish when we got to Al Asad and the perk of a nice scoff. We'll still be going to Camp Duhlab tomorrow and, fingers crossed, another quiet run back to Camp Victory, but the odds are against us.

The guys are in mixed moods but this is down to the other guys losing their jobs but the contract will be renewed in March so it won't be too long before they're back out here. Well, I'm just pleased to be going home in nine days and find time to relax, although I'll have the worry of being sent the brown letter e-mail saying that they've cut our team back and our jobs have gone will be on my mind. I think our team should be OK and it'll only be two months anyway before we'd be back, but if not, it'll be time to get the CV out again and try another company and probably end up in Africa or even Afghanistan again.

Looking forward to having a good night's sleep as I'll be on the gun tomorrow and it'll be bloody cold, I had the comfort of being vehicle commander today. Who knows, might get to shoot some bad guys down by Abu Ghraib tomorrow.

Me stood next to one of the old MIG's at Al Asad destroyed during the Gulf War.

03/01/07

It was a cold night and none of us were looking forward to getting up this morning, we had a lovely breakfast courtesy of the US military then went back to the Parson's 5 yard to meet the clients. We escorted the EOD team up to camp Duhlab where they would be staying for the next couple of months while they get rid of the ordnance scattered around the area.

The EOD team took their own Mamba vehicles which are fully armoured and were originally used in Africa, they take a blast well from underneath which makes them a practical vehicle to use in Iraq. When we arrived at Camp Duhlab, I noticed they had already started to set up the defence Hescos around the camp which would be used as their main defence line if they came under attack.

We were informed by one of the Parson's security guys that a Chechen sniper was operating in the area and had recently shot two US marines, hitting both in the neck. It's been quite common for Chechen Muslims to now be fighting in Iraq and Afghanistan and they are very efficient fighters. As we were leaving the INGs informed us they had caught two insurgents that have been responsible for a number of IED attacks in the area. After they had stopped, the INGs searched the vehicle and found maps of all ASP sites in the area which struck suspicion, they will now be dealt with by the US military.

We carried on down south towards Fallujah and then onto Abu Ghraib. At this point I became a little more alert expecting the worse to happen but to my surprise it was quiet, but by the look on the large IED crater, on our side of the road, we passed, I think we missed a loud bang. We carried on route until about two kilometres from our turn-off for Camp Victory but were delayed as the US military EOD team had discovered an IED so we had to wait for them to carry out a controlled explosion.

We finally got into Camp Victory but didn't have time for food, we did pick up some things from the PX though. On the drive out, I watched the sun setting as the full moon was starting to rise in the sky. We drove past one of the lakes that is in the camp and it was as still as a mill pond, I looked and enjoyed the moment of beauty before driving back out into the madness.

We're off up north again tomorrow calling at Camp Spiker and probably staying the night at Camp Buckmaster, I hope all our jobs are trouble free before I go on leave. The guys are needing a break and the recent job cuts have left the guys deflated but hopefully spirits will lift.

Les (TL) briefing the Parson's 5 EODT guys.

Clients Mambas.

Hescos surrounding the camp.

INGs with detained Insurgents on floor.

Waiting to set off to camp Victory just after the US military carried out a controlled explosion on the IED.

04/01/07

We had a busy day today, lots of clients and lots of things going on. Conrad (Team 47) joined our team for this task as Mick is going home on compassionate leave due to the death of his grandfather. We collected both Excursion vehicles from the Farm with clients then made our way through Baghdad heading for the north Tampa route. After about fifteen minutes into our journey, we came up to an IP checkpoint, as we had driven through the check-point I hear the sound of gunfire coming from the rear, I immediately called over the radio "Rounds fired at the rear."

I noticed Paul (Rear Gunner) slowly lowering his head and I thought, *That's a good idea I'll keep my head down*, another few rounds went off then we were out of range. From that point on it was a clear run all the way up to Camp Spiker and we didn't even have any trouble at Sammarra which is unusual. On the way up, we did notice, as we were passing Tikrit, that there was still a lot of people mourning Saddam Hussein's execution, there were convoys of vehicles with people with red and white shamags, some sitting on the tops of their cars carrying pictures of Saddam. As we passed, they angrily pointed flat palmed at us as if to say, "You your fault." But we noticed a definite hostility more than normal in the area.

We dropped our clients of at the Parson's yard at Camp Spiker then went to refuel, while at the fuel point, Paul and I were talking about a large cloud of smoke we could see in the distance behind us as we were both stood up in the pods looking out of the gunners hatch. As we both went to look forward we heard an enormous boom from an IED, it was probably the biggest IED I've ever seen here or in Afghanistan.

The IED had detonated about one kilometre from Camp Spiker and by the size of the blast, the insurgents had targeted a tank or some other large armoured vehicle, as the sheer size of the blast was unbelievable. After the blast went off, I noticed something fly into the air which was glowing red so it must have been some sort of large artillery shell or something, I would have been surprised that anyone would have survived such a large blast.

We started to make our way to the exit point of Camp Spiker as we had to call a Camp Buckmaster, as we were about to leave, we could hear the sirens of the emergency US military recovery team which indicated to me that a US military call sign had been hit by the IED. Les said if the clients were ready at camp

Buckmaster then there would be a chance of getting back to Baghdad today; our progress was delayed though due to a suspect IED near Tikrit.

The US military stopped us from progressing with journey so we stopped opposite Tikrit. After about five minutes I heard shots fired from the left, I said to Marcus over the radio, "Did you hear that?" he said.

"Yes, I did, mate." We then put all of our attention on the direction the gunfire came from, we noticed a large gathering of people opposite where we had stopped and they were taking a lot of interest in our vehicles. After about forty minutes the route was cleared and we continued our journey onto Camp Buckmaster. As we got near to our turn off point Les asked Baz, "Is this our turn off?"

Baz said, "No, we took the other one when we were with Shane."

When we arrived, we were to find out that the decision Les made about which junction to take was more important than he knows. We were told by one of the Parson's guys that the convoy team that was on its way to Buckmaster, had been hit by an IED as they turned of Tampa. It could have easily been us that were hit by the IED but the choice was made to go for the second route, luckily no one was hurt and the IED was quite small, all that it did was throw a lot of dirt up in the air.

As the clients weren't ready, Les chose to stay at Camp Buckmaster but at least we can have a hot shower, there isn't much here as the camp will be closing down soon.

Well I hope the route south tomorrow is clear and the bad guys don't come out to play, I will also be keeping my eyes on the small potholes after what happened to Baz and his last IED experience.

IED blast, seconds after detonating in the centre of the picture which was taken from Camp Spiker's fuel point.

Smoke rising high from the IED blast site.

05/01/07

It was a pretty easy day today as we only went to Camp Spiker then waited around to get information on what we would be doing. Les came back to brief us up on what was going on as he'd spoken to ops in Baghdad, he said we would be going back to camp Buckmaster then in the morning we would be taking five clients back to Baghdad with us. We stayed at Camp Spiker to have a tasty lunch then got some toiletries from the PX and finished things off with having a café latte at the Green Bean Café.

As we were sitting at the café, we noticed a change in the weather, it had been cold all day but we didn't expect a sandstorm then hailstones with a bit of rain of course. The weather isn't a problem as the UK weather is, just as bad except for the sandstorm but bad weather means no top cover (helicopter gun cover). Luckily the weather did clear and we made our way back down Tampa to Camp Buckmaster as we were travelling, I was thinking about what some of the guys were talking about, they had seen Jeremy Clarkson (*Top Gear*) on a video clip on YouTube website.

Clarkson had a turn at driving an armoured vehicle and drove the Tampa route, which is the most dangerous road in Iraq, as he's being filmed, he comes out with the comment, "I'm absolutely shitting myself," but that's the typical thing he'd do as he's a bit of a daredevil. It was an experience I suppose and as he was here to visit the troops at the time I take my hat off to him for trying the experience.

We arrived back at Camp Buckmaster relatively early and had a nice surprise, we were told that as Camp Buckmaster would be shutting down we could take whatever we wanted, including food, furniture, basically anything, not that we had the room in our vehicles. I couldn't believe how they would be shutting the camp down, they would be taking nothing, no equipment from the cookhouse, ablutions, accommodation everything is to be burnt to the ground.

It was such a surprise as there are hundreds of thousands of dollars, maybe close to a million, in the camp but that's the American way, no budget, what it must be to have such wealth. The food and water that people died for delivering, is to be destroyed and why not put it to some other use or give it to the local people, who knows there's no sense in stupidity. I've noticed our team has gained a good bond with one another although Ray, John (young) and Dave are never too keen to interact with the guys and outcast themselves, which is their own choice. I remember trying to get to know the guys and it wasn't easy to gain a place in the team and you have to prove your capable of being relied on, all I know now is that I'm glad to be in Team 46.

Our vehicles parked at the left side of Camp Buckmaster.

The right side of Camp Buckmaster with Paul in the bottom left of the picture, returning after doing a little shopping.

The water to be wasted after people had died delivering it seems a shame and a waste.

Food that will be destroyed, there's enough to feed a small army.

The cookhouse, all equipment and furniture to be burnt including cookers, microwaves, coffee makers and other cooking utensils.

06/01/07

We all had to be up early this morning at Camp Buckmaster as they were looking to set the first charges off at around 10.30 a.m., as we sat in the cookhouse, I realised that the biggest conversation starter is the weather and how much people mention it to start a conversation (most talked about subject in the world). We were able to get breakfast in the form of a cup of coffee and a serial bar which was better than nothing I suppose and I'm not too fussy at 5.30 a.m. in the morning. The guys had made sure they could load whatever they could into the vehicles before we left, we had new mattresses, one of the coffee makers, a new microwave, enough food to last a year, oh, and Baz took a single bed.

We set off at 9.30 a.m. and almost immediately were stopped by US military, they had just detonated an IED and were clearing the debris, the IED was placed at the Tikrit Arches. The Arches act as a good IED firing point as it's like putting your head into the lion's mouth, you have to travel through one of two arches and the structure can be seen at a distance which is good for the insurgent about to detonate it.

After the debris was cleared, we carried on with our route down south on Tampa, we had a clear run and no incidents, which was strange but a pleasant surprise but that might be due to the heavy presence of US military armoured vehicles we had seen on the way. We got to Camp Victory at around 1.30 p.m. and after calling for a bit of food we then made our way back to the Villas where we unloaded our hoard items from Buckmaster.

On returning, we found out that Team 44 had had a bad day yesterday as one of their convoy truck drivers was killed, the driver had been shot in the head near Taji in between Al Asad and Fallujah. Unfortunately, after the truck driver was shot, he lost control of his vehicle and crashed into a nearby garage killing a young boy who was unable to get out of the way in time. The strange thing is that the TL of Team 44 didn't know one of his trucks was missing, and they had to go back and get the body of the truck driver that had been recovered by the IP, the truck was stolen after it crashed.

I'm looking forward to leave now and having normality back for a short period of time and most of all to be with my loved ones.

Getting ready to set off from Camp Buckmaster.

Camp Buckmaster at its last dawn on the horizon.

Team 40 leaving with the convoy they're escorting back to Baghdad.

US military clearing debris away from where the IED detonated on the right side of the Tikrit Arches.

07/01/07

Last night's sleep seemed a little surreal as it was like when you're asleep and you're dreaming and you think it's real but last night what was happening was real. At around 2am I heard thumps then large explosions, insurgents had set up a mortar base plate (MBP) near our villa and were attacking the US military in the green zone. They were close as I could hear the mortars being fired then the explosion when the mortar had landed, this must have gone on for around thirty minutes but as I was sleepy, I was unsure.

There was the occasional burst of small arms fire as well so they meant business and it must have been well planned to get so close to their target.

We cleaned the chain ammunition for the Minimis today as the wet weather has made the links a bit tacky, a quick wipe over of around two thousand rounds with an oily rag and they should be as good as new. Just got to sort out our vehicle now then de-bomb our magazines and we're ready to pack bags and go. I'll leave my work kit here as I definitely won't need it back home.

Wiping the Minimi chain ammunition over with an oily rag, just lightly as not to cause a breach explosion, we did belts of two hundred 5.56mm, one in every five is a tracer round.

08/01/07
It's raining pretty bad today and as a result there's no top cover so Team 47 has been locked down at Al Asad for another day. They will probably get back tomorrow evening, weather permitting. Our team will be going to the BIAP (airport)

tomorrow to collect the guys from our team who were lucky enough to keep their jobs and return from leave.

I'll start packing my things tomorrow night after we've done our last short job to the airport so let's hope all goes well and it's nice and quiet.

We were informed today of information that had been gained by an intelligence source, that members of Jama'at al Tawhid wa'al Jihad (JTL) are marking vehicles used by insurgents with red tape and paint. A single piece of red tape is placed on the gas tank cover of the vehicle and a single red line of paint is placed on the hub cap of one wheel on each side of the vehicle, the previous colour used was green.

The markings are used so members of the JTJ will be able to recognise other members of the group, even if they do not know each other personally. JTJ members questioned as to why their vehicles are marked in such a way most likely will reply that the markings are simple decorations. This method of identification is used primarily in the Ta'meen district and in central Ramadi.

09/01/07

We got up early this morning thinking the airport run would go on time but three guys from Team 47 were still on their way back from Al Asad this morning so we were running late. Luckily they held the plane for an hour so the guys wouldn't miss their connecting flight in Kuwait. I couldn't help but think of Thursday when we would be flying out on leave and have a nice four week break.

Although the task was only to the BIAP (airport) it was still a little worrying as it was the last job I'd do before going on leave so I didn't want anything to happen, the news of small arms fire on the route this morning wasn't very comforting. While we drive down the dual carriageway, it would be so difficult to pinpoint a shooter as there are empty buildings, open roof tops, rubble and good cover positions which give excellent firing points to the opportunist gunmen.

We got to the airport, dropped the guys off and picked up Shane, Sammy, Nick and Paul, I think they know how lucky they are to have got back out after four of the guys lost their jobs. Our team will be going to ASP 7 and 8 tomorrow but me, Baz, Chris, Dave and Cammy will be left behind to finish packing and we have to hand our weapons into the armoury.

10/01/07

Our team had a good run to ASP 7 and 8 today and no trouble thankfully, this is my last entry now as I'll be going on leave tomorrow. I will be looking forward to time off but my thoughts will be with the guys in the team and that they stay safe.

08/02/07

Well got back from leave today and was told we've become a multi-task team, which means we'll be doing convoys as well as PSD work. The guys were hit six times out on their last task that's the joy of escorting large slow vehicles but that's part of the job I suppose. Marcus said the team fired over a thousand rounds during the contact, he also said it was initiated by RPG fire (Rocket Propelled Grenade).

I'm going to sort my kit out this evening and fit the new laser sight to my M4. It seems strange to be back but also as if I only left yesterday but I remember that leave was different this time and as I met someone, it was all the more difficult to return.

Coming back isn't easy, it never is and it's only made easy by seeing the bank statement at the end of the month.

09/02/07

Cammy, Derek and Mick were spammed to join another team for a couple of days to do a run ten kilometres outside Baghdad, they were ambushed on the way back and one of their trucks was destroyed so they're not looking forward to tomorrow's journey. Cammy said his vehicle was hit three times and a lot of smoke was coming in the vehicle, most importantly, no one was hurt.

It has got so much worse recently and the insurgents seem to be more confident than ever. We will do our first task on Monday but it shouldn't be too bad as it's only to Camp Victory. Well, we had a bit of humour today at around lunch time I heard laughing out by the TV room, I went to see what was going on and found Baz's room covered in white fire extinguisher powder. The plug socket in his room had caught fire and flames were coming out from the wall, aahh, I've missed the villa, 'not', it most definitely reminds me of that film with Tom Hanks and Shelley Long, in *The Money Pit* where the house is a wreck (probably in better shape than our villa though).

10/02/07

Got an early call from Shane this morning as we had to go and escort one of the Parson's trucks back to Camp Victory as it had broken one of its axles and the trailer was travelling sideways down the road. I've gone on to rear gunner which means I control the traffic at the rear of our team's vehicle and make sure they hold back.

This was put to the test today as we had to wait to go into Camp Victory, a white sedan car and other vehicles were pushing too close, I give the driver a clenched fist to indicate to him that I wanted him to stop. He didn't bother to stop so I quickly positioned the Minimi machine gun in his direction as if to fire, he slammed his brakes on so quickly that the truck behind him smashed into the rear of his vehicle. After a short while, I was told by Les to let the vehicles through, the sedan driver gave me a good stinking disgusted look as if to say, "You, bastard." It's for our benefit as suicide bombers mostly use cars out here so shoot first before it's too late.

I'm sure worse is to come, no doubt, as the rear vehicle is the one that takes the most gunfire and IEDs but at least if we do any convoy work they'll go for the big trucks first. The guys are getting on much better now that Team 47 has gone from our villa and there is good camaraderie amongst the lads. Phoned the family to let them know I'm OK, back to the routine of letting them know I'll be out on task for a few days and then ringing them to tell them I got back OK. What Dawn texted me meant a lot. She said stay safe and come back as I worry about you and its only one brother I've got, comments like that are priceless and mean the world. It was strange to be out again today feeling the risk and having the danger around, it brings an instant alertness alive in me.

Well looks like a DVD tonight and a chilled evening, back to quiet, lonely evening with memories of the last four weeks to keep me going to next leave, ah, how the little things mean so much. People take things for granted if only they could see the other side of life, the love, hatred, hurt, death, suffering, pain. I spoke to Izrah (villa cleaning lady) today and noticed she was dressed all in black, I knew her mother was ill before I went on leave but, unfortunately, she died a day ago and had been suffering for a few months. Maybe if they had the resources would she still be alive now but this is something I've seen before except it was a small Afghan boy that was dead in his father's arms.

11/02/07

Me, Baz, Chris, Dave and Shane went into the green zone today so we could collect some water and food from the PX, we'll do a big shop tomorrow when we go for our biometrics at Camp Victory. Shane went to meet his ammo contact while we were in the PX for the exchange of a couple of bottles of fire water (whiskey) he got some fragmentation grenades, smoke grenades, phosphorous grenades, 5,000 rounds of ammunition and new Minimi ammo belt bags.

We heard of some trouble that happened yesterday where five IPs (Iraqi police) were killed during an attack by insurgents on their base, they publicly beheaded one in front of a crowd. We'll be going out on a long job on Wednesday; we'll probably get a brief off Shane on Tuesday.

12/02/07

John and Marcus and some of the other lads will be going on their four weeks leave tomorrow so their morale is high, I'm already looking forward to my next leave well, at least I'll have the room all to myself. The biometrics went OK today, we had our pictures and fingerprints taken, felt more like a criminal line-up instead of an ID card application.

We got our usual grief treatment of the grumpy US sergeant, he just hates the fact we get paid more than him, he is one of the most arrogant people I've ever met.

The guys will be leaving at nine a.m. tomorrow, one of the other teams will be dropping them off at the BIAP. It looks like it'll be a quiet day tomorrow but I think we're off up north to Al Asad on Wednesday, so we may be in for some fun and games.

13/02/07

It's been a quiet day today just did some training after saying farewell to the guys going on leave. I managed to get my hands on a scope sight for my M4 and good old Roy (armourer) fitted it for me and bore sighted the sight for me. Going to pack my kit for tomorrow's job up to Al Asad.

14/02/07

It's Valentine's Day today but I don't think I'll be getting any cards out here, but never mind, it's what's in the heart that counts. We got up early this morning as we needed to go to Camp Victory and collect five clients and three trucks; strangely enough we got into the camp without any fuss. We had a brief off Shane then headed for the west exit, we had a feeling we would be hit today as trucks are easy targets and we were to be proven right.

As we were coming up to Abu Ghraib, we heard the loud familiar boom of an IED. As I looked in my side mirror, I could see a large cloud of smoke rise from the rear of the convoy. The IED was initiated level with one of the trucks but it went off a little early and managed to catch the front of the second truck smashing the front and side window and causing some body damage to the cab of the vehicle. Luckily the vehicle wasn't immobilised and the driver wasn't hurt so we could continue on our journey.

We got to Camp Duhlab at about lunch time and left the trucks there as they will need to be unloaded, we will call at Camp Duhlab in the morning to escort the trucks back to Baghdad. Before we left Camp Duhlab we were told that this morning an insurgent had infiltrated the IP camp (Iraqi police) and shot one of them killing him instantly. Although they have IP outside the Duhlab compound and a perimeter of Hesco's it is still a high-risk area where they are vulnerable to insurgent attacks and IDF (Indirect Fire). Well, quiet DVD night in the transit tent tonight, and then up early for breakfast before meeting the trucks to drive down south.

Parson Truck with IED damage.

15/02/07

We got up nice and early this morning in order to get a nice breakfast before going to Camp Duhlab then Baghdad, we all were chuckling about Nick screaming out in his sleep he shouted "You bitch," so God knows, women problems no doubt. After breakfast we took some clients to Camp Duhlab, when we arrived we made sure the trucks were loaded and ready to leave on time.

At no surprise, one of the drivers was loading some tyres on the back of his flat-bed which delayed us slightly which was fortunate. As we were about to leave, I noticed one of the ratchet straps on the flat-bed had come loose. I stopped the truck so Chris and I could get out to assist the driver to secure the straps. As we were doing the straps we heard a loud boom in the direction of the main road towards our exit point.

A suicide bomber VBIED (Vehicle Bomb Improvised Explosive Device) had driven to the junction to meet us but as we were delayed, when he got there, he had nothing to bomb, for some reason he detonated the bomb killing himself instantly. There wasn't anything much left but a burnt-out shell that was a car and bits of the bomber cooking in the fire, luckily none of the IPs or EODT security guys were injured.

The US military came and did an analysis of the site to get information about the blast and device but the worrying thing is, how did they know our movements and why we were specifically targeted and they knew we were leaving the camp — how? We'll just need to keep our eyes open and be wary of cars that get too close for comfort, I can't understand what would make a person get up in the morning and decide to go and blow himself up.

After the US marines had cleared the area, we escorted the trucks and the client Excursion vehicle out of Camp Duhlab towards the main road, as we approached the main road, we could see the debris from the bomb blast. The EODT security team were by the junction to clear our exit, as we were coming to the junction I noticed a car approaching from the left. The IP signalled the car to pull over at the side of the road to let us pass but as he drove off the tar road there was a flash and loud boom, it was unbelievable and tragic as the driver had hit a PIED (Pressure Plate Improvised Explosive Device). One minute the car was there, the next it had turned into a burning shell and what was left of the poor driver. It was a shock to think that all of our vehicles had driven around the IED and not even known it was there on the way in to Camp Duhlab.

We carried on after the incident as we had already lost three hours at Camp Duhlab and we needed to make good time, Uranium wasn't to be so forgiving though. As we approached the end of Uranium, just before it joins the Bronze route, we were stopped by a US military EODT team who were doing controlled detonations on a few IEDs. We were held up again by IEDs, one at Falujah and the other by Abu Ghraib, not to mention the slow-moving military convoys. — mind numbing.

We left Al Asad at 08.30 hours and didn't arrive in Camp Victory until 02.15 hours which meant we'd taken over seventeen hours to do a two-and-a-half hour journey. There was a large number of convoys on the road and the US military are very twitchy and nervous and would probably shoot anyone they're not certain about. Well, a well earnt day off tomorrow the following day I think we are going to ASP 7 and 8 so should be a quiet trip.

Team 46 just before we're about to leave for Camp Duhlab.

Smoke rising from the horizon where the suicide bomber's car exploded near the exit point.

What's left of the bomber car pushed off the main road.

Shane was shown the bomb scene on the Eagle Eye screen.

Smoke rising from an IED detonated by the US EODT team on Uranium.

16/02/07

It's a visit to ASP 7 and 8 tomorrow, so hopefully it'll be its usual quiet run down south, it's been a casual day today just got some admin done and my regular visit to the gym. Team 45 got hit by a large IED today, one of the expat guys was knocked unconscious but there were no serious casualties, surely, they must be running out of explosives by now for the amount of IEDs they plant on the roads.

17/02/07

Got up this morning feeling like the back end of a bus as my stomach was aching and I was feeling sick, after getting up I had to run to the toilet and after dressing I went a second time to be sick. Good old Iraqi hygiene, no matter what, after leave and coming back, you're bound to get a case of the shits you've just got to hope it's gone in a day or so as it can just drain the energy out of you.

I was gunner in the rear vehicle today so at least I could get plenty of fresh air; I suffered most of the day and couldn't risk eating so I just sipped water all day. Every time we got to our location I was lying down as I was feeling so sick but this isn't a place to whimp out, I was straight back to my feet when we were ready to go as there's no sick chits issued out here.

The journey went well as expected and we had no incidents, which was a relief for the way I was feeling, although we did see a lot of new IED holes on route so the insurgents had been working in the area. After we had returned some clients back to the farm at the end of the day, we went for a De Frac meal, on my way in I noticed some US soldiers making fun of our 'Pig' armoured vehicle saying it had to be wound up to go like some clockwork toy. I couldn't resist but say to them, "Yes, it might be a wind-up vehicle but we can do our job well and we still get paid more than you guys."

Americans, they have all the gear and no idea they live in a world where they are the best and everyone else in the world is second, not so I'd say. Shane said we've got the next few days off so good wind down time. We'll be going to the BIAP tomorrow thought to collect our MNFI cards and do some shopping at the PX.

18/02/07

I'm feeling a lot better today and we had the extra bonus of having a lie-in this morning as we're going to the BIAP tomorrow now. I'll go to the gym and do some weights today and leave the running as I don't want to tempt fate and be ill again, it looks like our next job will be on Wednesday so we'll just have to wait out for Shane's brief.

Spoke to Martyn in the gym, he said that Kev was hurt badly after the blast the other day. Kev's hatch on his Armadillo armoured vehicle was blown shut by an IED on top of his head giving him severe head injuries. Kev has had two operations on his head and has been flown to Germany. Martyn said he still hasn't recovered consciousness, I hope he'll be OK.

19/02/07

Well we finally got our MNFI ID cards which means we can get access to anywhere on Camp Victory. We had a good shop at the PX which was well needed as I had run out food. We've got an airport run tomorrow so it'll be an easy day just the BIAP and back tomorrow.

20/02/07

We did the airport run today and picked up some of the guys from Team 43, its always the same for the guys, it feels as if you've never left this place and leave goes so quick. We brought everyone back to the Villas and prepared the vehicles for tomorrow as we're off to Camp Arlington to drop off some clients. So tomorrow we could be seeing some action as it's been quite nasty on the route out west and some RPG (Rocket Propelled Grenade) fire as well as SAF (Small Arms Fire).

21/02/07

What a crazy day, or more of a blur I should say, it started off by us being told we'd be going to Camp Summerall and not Camp Arlington to drop clients off. We knew there was a strong possibility of being attacked today as the north route is the worse to travel. As we were travelling past Mushada, we were beginning to think we were going to have a good drive through but as soon as that thought had passed my mind, there was the sound of bullets cracking over our vehicles and the immediate sound of top gunners returning fire.

The people around us were running for their lives and taking cover behind anything thicker than a piece of paper. The panic on their faces was so obvious as the gun battle carried on until we had travelled out of the insurgents line of fire. There were only a few gunmen and they were hidden down one of the side streets, randomly shooting from good cover and they were successful in hitting our vehicles. Shane and Baz's vehicles took some direct hits, but the damage was only minor. After the contact with the insurgents we were soon held up by US military EODT carrying out a controlled explosion on an IED that had been found, when we stopped we quickly checked our vehicles for damage.

We got the clients to Sommerall on good time we were then told by Shane that we'd be calling at Camp Spiker to meet another call sign Team 74. Team 74 had taken a bad hit and lost three vehicles and had one injured local national so they would require us to bring up the rear of their convoy. We knew we were going to be a target that day as there were ten trucks which give the insurgents plenty to shoot at. We lined the vehicles up and made our way onto Tampa south bound and kept to a steady hundred kilometres an hour so we'd keep good time.

We had been briefed earlier about a number of cars that had been set up as VBIEDs (Vehicle Bomb Improvised Explosive

Device) and to be careful of parked cars. As we were approaching Mutlaq Nayif, we heard a call over the radio that one of our teams had engaged a car that was acting suspiciously. It was believed that the car was being used by insurgents who intended to detonate IEDs, the car got shot pretty bad by the team and by the time we passed I don't think any insurgents would have lived through the bullets and fire (which isn't so bad).

After we passed the burning car, we were stopped once again by the US military EODT but after a short while the convoy was moving again. We actually thought we'd get back through Mushada incident free, how wrong could we have been, as Chris and I were in discussion we were giving the sudden shock of the top gunners shooting again.

I could see bullets hitting the ground around our vehicle in a continuous flow. I looked towards a field opposite our vehicle and saw a lone Iraqi farmer standing by his sheep and bullets were even hitting the ground near him. The insurgents were firing from our rear right and were trying to immobilise one of our vehicles or one of the trucks, thankfully the gunners returned fire quickly and got the Insurgents to slow their rate of fire.

Unfortunately, some of the truck drivers panicked when bullets hit their truck. Ss they approached an American checkpoint, one of the truck drivers lost his vision due to dust being kicked up by other vehicles. The driver came into the checkpoint too quickly and smashed into a ten-ton concrete blast barrier and was smashed up pretty bad; the truck had to be pulled out of the checkpoint by a US Bradley tank. The driver was seriously hurt and broke his pelvis; a US medic Black Hawk helicopter flew in and took the injured drive to the Baghdad hospital.

I must admit there was a sense of excitement about seeing so much action in one day but also mentally draining as well, although Baz was soon into his cigars having a Hamlet moment and the smokers amongst the guys must have done a packet easy today. It doesn't seem like reality in a sense that some people were shooting at us to kill us today and my hands have stopped shaking now so have Chris's I think, but through it all we still managed to laugh.

Team 74's vehicle with IED damage.

Burnt out shell is all that is left of the insurgent's car.

Black Hawk helicopter come to collect injured truck driver.

Truck showing heavy signs of the collision with the ten-ton blast barrier.

22/02/07

Well, the guys are on a bit of a come down after yesterday's excitement, it brings reality home, often I wonder after a dangerous day, what would life be like back home for my friends and family if their world didn't have an Anthony in it. I really need to consider my future and when should I settle back home and concentrate on my life. I just hope there's something special there for me and on leave.

We're off to Al Asad tomorrow, escorting three trucks so it could be an interesting day, I'd rather it be a quiet day but who knows. I was told today that I'll be driving a PLS for Team 45 on Sunday, we're going on a four-day mission up to the Iraq/Kurdistan border. I'm not happy being a sitting duck but I may as well get on with it as I won't be doing this forever and they should get their own PLS drivers soon.

Well, going to get packed ready for time away then a good cup of tea before chilling this evening.

23/02/07

Unexpectantly, we got to Camp Duhlab and Al Asad without any incidents although, we we're stuck at Camp Duhlab longer than thought as we had to wait for the Eagle Eye to be replaced and mounted onto one of the trucks. We got into Al Asad at around eight p.m. and I wasted no time in getting a well-deserved shower, another night in the Parson's tent (deep joy).

Shane (TL) and I at Camp Duhlab.

24/02/07

We had a free run back from Al Asad which meant no trucks to escort or clients, so foot down all the way. We were making good time and seemed to be running into very few US military convoys. Chris like's the odd cigarette in the vehicle so I have to let the window down so I can get some fresh air in 'bloody smokers', we were talking about the good old MOD days and the pop group, Madness, who were amazing at the time.

We were approaching Fallujah and Chris decided to have a cigarette, just as he was about to light it, I lowered my window slightly to let some fresh air, suddenly 'boom' our vehicle was rocked by an IED. My ears were aching straight away and a constant humming sound came to my head and the side of my face was stinging, from the flash of the blast. The dust inside the vehicle was everywhere and we could hardly see as it had been unsettled by the blast, my hands were shaking and I looked to Chris, we asked one another if we were OK. I looked down at my legs and felt my side by the door to see if I was bleeding but everything seemed OK.

Our wing mirror had been blown off and our radio antenna but otherwise the vehicle was OK except for a flat tyre from the blast. Cammy came alongside our vehicle as we were driving out of the contact blast and checked to see if our vehicle was OK. My face was stinging from the blast especially on the left side. I went deaf in my left ear and if it hadn't been for my radio ear-piece I may have lost it permanently, we got through the blast but my left ear was aching and I'd be lying if I didn't say it shook me. I must say my life did flash before my eyes but if the IED bomb was bigger, it could have been a different story but Chris and I are here to talk about it and we came through unharmed. Well I won't be using the phone for a couple of days until my hearing is OK again and my head feels a little better. I went for a check-up after and the doctor said my eardrum wasn't perforated and my hearing will return to normal — phew.

Recently IEDd Aiges vehicle where four people were killed on Uranium.

US Military IED sweeper on Uranium.

25/02/07

We got to Camp Sommerall (K2) nice and early and even had a trouble free run on the north Tampa road, although we did see an IED go off on the opposite side of the road while US Military convoy was going past. I was gunner in the second PLS with Ian and although he lost the wing mirror of the PLS he did OK except for hugging the side of the road which isn't a good thing for IEDs. It was noticeable that as we were in Armadillo armoured vehicles and two PLSs, we looked more like an American convoy and we just passed everything.

We'll do a drop to Camp Jaguar tomorrow so it looks like we'll be staying at Camp Arlington for at least two nights.

26/02/07

We went up to Camp Jaguar today to collect two Iso containers, the journey up north took us past the IED point where Kev was injured, so the guys were on their toes. On the way up we passed a graveyard of petrol and oil tankers that had been destroyed either by insurgents or IP who didn't get their protection money off the tanker drivers. I will be driving a PLS tomorrow but I'm glad, as Ian's driving makes me nervous, he is not made for this type of work.

Ian found it difficult to take direction today when I was trying to guide him when he was off-loading, I'm sure he still thinks he's an RSM (Regimental Sergeant Major). He just got on my nerves today, he loves hugging the side of the road and hitting every pothole but I'm sure he'd stop if an IED hit his vehicle for the first time. Well we'll see how he gets on tomorrow. Ian is the type of person that likes to put his own incompetence onto others.

Well, Team 45 work well except for one rotten egg, Tank, an ex 2 RAF Regt guy thinks he's a Navy Seal or something oh and the fact he has had an ND (Negligent Discharge) which is firing a bullet by accident. Oh, and there was the time he was meant to be low profile in Baghdad and got out of his vehicle to stop traffic with his weapon showing, what a fool.

Well, only a short run down to Camp Spiker so it should be an early finish hopefully.

Ian at the wheel of the PLS.

27/02/07

It was a nice steady day today and a bit quicker as I was operating the PLS today. We picked up two containers then left them on the vehicles for our long drive up to Zakho tomorrow.

I'm hoping it'll be a quiet run but you can never tell in this game, I'm going to have a well-earned shower now then have some food probably watch a DVD as well. Well no point in blabbing on as nothing much happened today except Dave, Ian and Jason leaving their weapon, helmet, body armour and other kit in the PLSs when leaving Camp Arlington, they must have forgotten we're in Iraq

Jordie seems a bit different lately, although it's been a while since I have seen him or it could be to do with his shooting incident last month. Team 45 were travelling up to Camp Jaguar last month, it was early in the morning and there was fog everywhere. They were about six miles north of Camp Sommerall, as they were coming around a bend, Jordie noticed two men in the road and they were carrying AKs. Jordie realised they were insurgents laying an IED bomb.

He fired some warning shots but they ran, he fired again killing one of the men, the other threw his weapon down, the team just carried on with their journey after the incident but it was Jordie's first kill, but not to be his last.

28/02/07

Well it was a long journey today and not made easier by having a faulty PLS truck, with all the billions of dollars the Parson's company is worth you'd think they'd get their trucks sorted. We went to collect the extra PLS and containers containing explosives for the EODT in Zakho but found that the spare PLS was in shit state, it had no spare wheel and the rear back tyre wouldn't inflate. I thought they had fixed the tyre and managed to travel twenty kilometres before it went flat again.

Shortly after this, we were IEDd. The IED bomb detonated opposite John's (2 i/c Team 45) vehicle but did no damage.

I told Danny I would carry on as the vehicle didn't have a load but soon after, the tyre gained some heat and exploded there were pieces of rubber flying off everywhere. Fortunately, the wheel rim didn't touch the floor. I managed to make it to Mosul and checked the vehicle over, I didn't see a problem in continuing on with the journey and it would be a better option than leaving the vehicle or destroying it.

Dave had a few bad memories brought back when we arrived at Mosul as he was shot there March 9th 2004 while doing PSD work, he was shot in the elbow and shoulder but luckily it wasn't to serious and he lived. Dave described being shot as if he'd been scolded by a hot poker, not that I'd ever want to experience that as having them crack above my head is bad enough.

The scenery up north Iraq was beautiful and the northern mountains, bordering Turkey, were covered in snow, the Kurds were very friendly and seemed better organised with their lifestyle than the Iraqis in the south, we even took our weapons down and took our body armour off. There is no love lost between the Kurds and the Iraqis as the Kurds suffered badly during Saddam's rule. After dropping the PLS and explosives off, we all went to stay at a Kurdish hotel, it was very cheap and we all enjoyed the bonus of having clean sheets and a hot shower.

In the evening, we had a few sociable drinks and all sat round sharing stories from the past. Team 45 have good camaraderie amongst their team which is good and they seemed to have bonded well. After a late finish, we all went to bed except for Derek and Jordie, they pushed on a bit later so their heads will be banging in the morning.

I travelled over a hundred and fifty miles like this.

Coming into Mosul.

Travelling through the busy and dangerous streets of Mosul.

Arriving at Zakho.

At the hotel bar in Zakho with the lads, Mick (left, hotel waiter, Jordie (front), me, Tomo (back) and local Kurd.

Dave's smile hiding the pain of being bounced around in the PLS.

01/03/07

We had a nice breakfast this morning and left the hotel at about 08.30 a.m. Derek looked a bit rough as I predicted but soon recovered after a cat-nap before we got back to the danger zone. The PLSs had no loads on the way back from Zakho so we made good time on our return journey, plus it was all downhill. I was impressed by Ian driving as he has no HGV so I give him respect in that sense, as he drives the PLS well, mind, we were bounced round all over the place because the back ends of the PLSs were light.

We travelled back without any incidents today, except for the US EODT detonating an IED which is a regular occurrence now. We went to Camp Arlington to collect four soft-skin F350 which had been loaded on to flat racks and trailers of course we had a few problems but soon sorted them out. Well, check e-mails later then chill just wondering if we'll get hit in Mushada on the way back down south tomorrow, we'll just have to wait and see.

02/03/07

We set off on time this morning from Camp Sommerall and had a very quiet run down south to Baghdad and we didn't even get any trouble going through Mushada. We got back to the Farm at Camp Victory and got showered, did our washing. Mick, Dave, Derrick and I will be going back to the Villa's tomorrow but best not hold our breath as were going out on a job on Monday and they need the PLSs.

Hopefully tomorrow we'll know if the job is still on for Monday, off to the gym with Mick after, looks like it's a DVD tonight.

03/03/07

It was nice to get back to the Villas and get some admin done and to get a good training session done as well. We're going to Camp Arlington tomorrow to escort ten Parson's trucks so it looks like we'll be staying the night at Camp Sommerall as they won't be able to unload the trucks until Monday.

We will be going straight to ASP 8 when we leave Camp Arlington tomorrow so it's going to be a long drive, just hope we don't attract too much attention with all the big trucks that look more like targets.

04/03/07

We got off at around 09.30 a.m. this morning, and as it was busy in Baghdad this morning, we were held up a lot. Just as expected, we were attacked in Mushada just some SAF (Small Arms Fire), it was obvious to see they were targeting the trucks hoping to immobilise one of them to make us stop and fight. The local people knew we were going to be attacked as they started running before the bullets started flying but that's normally the case, locals hiding the insurgents.

We were out of the contact after a couple of hundred metres and made sure none of the drivers were hurt. We carried on with the journey making good time but one of the trucks got IEDd on the Sammarra bypass, luckily the vehicle didn't sustain any serious damage. Well, tomorrow's journey to ASP 8 should be an interesting one as we have to pass through Mushada again and the other red spots, so we may be in for more fun and games.

05/03/07

We got up nice and early this morning ready for our crawl down to ASP 8. We started our journey at eight a.m. and finished this evening at nine p.m. We were surprised to get through Mushada without being attacked but by the looks of things the US military had been hit before we got there. Our convoy had to wait for one IED to be cleared and that was about it for the first half of our journey.

The trucks were carrying explosives today which would be used by the EODT guys at ASP 8 to destroy unexploded ordnance. If the first two trucks were hit in an attack or immobilised they would have to be destroyed by Apache helicopters so we marked the top of them with white crosses. Luckily it didn't have to come to that today and the drivers did well to keep things rolling but I think the insurgents in Mushada would have been put off as we fired rocket flares into the reeds to set them on fire, as not to give the bad guys a hiding place.

On the way I was surprised at how long the Iraqi's queue for fuel, we complain about a few cars been in front of us back home and they wait in a queue about half a mile long. We were slowed down coming through Baghdad as the traffic was really bad so it was a bit of driving down the wrong side of the road that got us through in the end. It was the Mardi militia's pilgrimage today, the men, women and children walk for days down south to Kabula to worship so it caused another hold up for us.

There were people still walking this evening and they'll probably be going all night but they have got plenty of rest tents on the way so people can sleep and have refreshments. After the trucks are off-loaded in the morning we will be making our way back up north to Baghdad so I'm hoping it won't take long as I just want to get back to the villa and have some down time.

Our truck's waiting to go over the Samarra Bridge where we were IEDd yesterday.

Reeds well alight after a rocket flare was fired into them.

Pushing through the rush hour traffic in Baghdad.

Mardi militia pilgrimage.

06/03/07

I had a good sleep last night even though it was blowing a gale and I was on a camp bed. We were up early for no reason as they took four hours to unload the trucks. We left ASP 8 at around 2.30 p.m. and made our way slowly down route Kiev as the pilgrims were on their second day of walking to Kabula.

We heard some bad news as well today, eighty-two pilgrims were killed by insurgents today while they were on their way to Kabula, forty-two thought they were going into a rest tent but were executed and the others were shot on the roadside. There is a lot of IP and ING (Iraqi National Guard) doing security on the pilgrim march but it doesn't seem to be enough to stop them from being killed.

We've got a couple of days off so I'm going to have a well-earned lie-in bed in the morning, I was nodding a bit today, as the last fourteen days have caught up with me.

Passing pilgrims on Route Kiev as they walk to Kabula.

Passing one of the rest tents at the side of the road where pilgrims can rest and have food and water.

07/03/07

It was so nice to have a late lie in this morning, after doing fourteen days non-stop I needed it, mind hopefully I can have another one tomorrow as long as we don't get a fast ball. Well, I just chilled today and even did a bit of sunbathing; the Villa could easily pass for a holiday resort if it wasn't for the loud bangs of bombs and the sound of guns been fired.

I went to the gym for my afternoon session as usual and a strange thing happened, I saw a lock bolt on the floor. The thought took me straight back to when my father helped me set up my storeroom for my business, Leaps and Bounds, at Craig-Y-Nos Castle; he used the bolts to fit the storeroom doors. He was amazing with his hands but he always was a good workman and could put his hand to anything, it's so strange how the smallest of things can bring vivid memories back to you (I miss you, Dad).

We haven't got anything on tomorrow but I expect we'll be out on the weekend if not on Friday but we'll soon be told no doubt.

08/03/07

It looks like we'll be out tomorrow as there has been an accident at ASP 8, the EOD Team were planning to do a controlled explosion to destroy one hundred and ten tons of ordnance (artillery shells and other bombs). Unfortunately, one of the EODT guys was killed today and two others injured, we're not sure who, so hopefully it's not Chuck or Shaun who we see on a regular basis at the camp.

We will be going to Camp Victory in the morning at 5am to collect the Excursion vehicle as we will need to bring the injured guys back. Cammy is going to empty the back of his armoured pod so the dead body can be placed there for the return journey then it will be taken to the morgue at Camp Striker in Baghdad. It looks like there must have been a premature detonation or the guys were too close but I'm sure we'll get the full story tomorrow when we get to ASP 8 The SOC Team (Scene of Crime) flew down by helicopter today to investigate what went wrong, so hopefully a clear picture will emerge on how the guy lost his life.

09/03/07

I didn't like getting up at four a.m. this morning and the journey to ASP 8 became a struggle to stay awake. We collected the EODT investigation team from the Farm before we left for ASP 8 and as we were taking them we had to stick to the 50 mph rule, mind numbing speed. When we got there we soon found out that it was a guy called Don who was killed, I had seen him down ASP 8 on a number of occasions.

Don was in his fifties and had a family so the mood at ASP 8 was very low and a few people were still in shock after Don's death. It seemed to be a freak accident but the EOD guys have a dangerous job working with sensitive explosives and Don had paid the ultimate price. It seems Don was preparing a number of 105mm artillery shells to be destroyed by using explosives, at some point one of the 105mm shells exploded prematurely while Don was working on it. We later found out that Don had been hitting the 105mm artillery shell with a hammer to loosen something which was the wrong thing to do to a sensitive explosive that had been bombed and sitting out in the sun.

Don took the full force of the blast. His clothes were completely blown off. He lost part of the side of his head and his left hand. He was killed instantly so at least it would have been quick. Two of his colleagues were also seriously injured and are recovering in hospital. They put Don's body in the refrigeration container at ASP 8 overnight until we got there this morning.

When we got there, the investigation team went out to see where Don was killed and to try and put together what happened. When they returned, we got Don's body out of the refrigeration container and put him into the back of Cammy's vehicle. The camp doctor came and put around twenty frozen bottles of water inside Don's body bag to keep him cool on the journey back to Baghdad until we could get him to the morgue at Camp Striker.

It was hard today as we were all in the same frame of mind about the situation and as me and Cammy discussed, how would our family feel if it was one of us in the body bag. I don't ever want to be in that situation, it seems so surreal to see a lifeless body of someone who was breathing, walking and talking just a day ago when we were down at ASP 8 and now he was lifeless and dead.

10/03/07

I felt a little rough this morning as I had a few drinks last night after our long day collecting Don's body. Baz, Cammy and I had a good chat in the TV room today, we were discussing about when Baz was serving with 2 Para in the Falklands War and when he landed in Bluff Cove. Baz was describing how a lot of soldiers suffered from post-traumatic stress disorder and how certain things in our memory trigger our flash backs.

The things we see, whether they are horrific or sad etc, they will always be part of our subconscious mind and when you see some things, they are engraved on your memory for all time. The only worrying thing is what memories are to come and how will I cope, only time will tell I suppose. I have to deal with what I've seen but I will always have my own flashbacks and low points. Well, another day off tomorrow and then off to ASP 7 on Monday so it should be a quiet run.

11/03/07

We had a fast ball today as one of Team 45s vehicles lost a wheel on the way in to Baghdad so we had to escort a recovery vehicle to the breakdown point. It all went smooth and we returned to the Villas after having food at Camp Victory. We're going to ASP 7 and ASP 8 tomorrow so it will be another journey down south. Getting itchy feet now, thinking about leave but I'm trying not to think about it too much as it will only make the days go slower.

12/03/07

It was a nice fast PSD run today and we managed to call at both ASP 7 and ASP 8 and still get back to Camp Victory for 3.30 p.m. There weren't any problems on our way down or on the way back, we brought some of the AGI lads back from ASP 8 as they're going on leave on Thursday with some of the guys from our team. The guys are on a high, obviously, as its just days away and they deserve it.

The rest of our team has to accompany Team 45 tomorrow up north as half of their team will be going on leave as well; I think they need us to drive some vehicles that need to be collected. The only thing with tomorrow's journey is Mushada, that place is hot with trouble and we've been told the insurgents are using armour piercing rounds; hopefully it'll be a quiet journey.

We're going to Al Asad on Wednesday so it looks like we're in for a busy week, I've noticed that the guys on my rotation are needing a break as well, as I can see the frustration and stress showing now.

Mick taking a break on the gun turret at ASP 7.

Shane, Baz, Mick, Nick, Sammy and Neil in the chat mingle taking the piss out of one another as usual.

13/03/07

It was another surprising run up north and back today although we had seen numerous large IED holes which looked fresh. We escorted two trucks and were meant to bring back three armoured Panther vehicles, except mine broke down before I left the camp. Going to Al Asad via Camp Duhlab so another long roll up Uranium.

14/03/07

It was a pleasant drive up north today, trouble free, and even Uranium wasn't too busy with convoys either. We got to Duhlab just before lunch and were greeted by the wreckage of a crashed helicopter. We found out that yesterday the Hip helicopter tried to take off but took too much dust into the engine causing it to stall; the helicopter just fell like a stone. Unbelievably, nobody was killed although the co-pilot broke his legs and was seriously injured, the pilot was OK and several Iraqi nationals survived as well.

After Duhlab, we took a Parson's client to Camp Wolf, the camp has grown in size since we last visited as there seems to be a lot of work going on there. We passed a tanker that had been IEDd on our way to Camp Wolf. It had been destroyed by the blast as the fuel tanks had caught fire. One of the other teams said it was a pressure plate IED or maybe a mine, luckily the tanker was carrying water and not fuel, that's probably why the driver walked away without being harmed.

We're escorting two trucks back to Baghdad tomorrow. They'll be going from Camp Duhlab. The truckss will be carrying Eagle Eye as far as I know, well it might make our return journey more interesting as the insurgents like to take a few shots at the truckss, but we'll just have to wait and see.

Hip Helicopter after it crashed.

Most of the impact was taken on the front of the nose of the helicopter.

15/03/07

Well we weren't held up for too long on Uranium on the way back from Al Asad and we didn't need to call at Camp Duhlab so we saved ourselves some time. We had no small arms fire or IEDs on our way back and it was relatively quiet all the way, which was a nice break although I struggled with the sleep monster as loud snoring kept me awake last night. Baz and Ray really do need to seek medical advice as it's just not normal to sound like a freight train when you're sleeping.

Mick taking a toilet stop on Uranium while Dave keeps a watchful eye for insurgents so Mick doesn't get anything shot off.

We got to Camp Victory at around 2.30 p.m. so we did a little shopping at the PX but I usually spend most of my time dragging Mick away from talking to the American female soldiers, but he's polite and just takes the piss mostly. After shopping, we came back to the villas and unpacked, the lads and I on our rotation can now officially start the countdown to our leave, four weeks today flying out — yippee.

Local Iraqi nationals working for Armor Group taking time out to play a game of football, not sure about the goalkeepers shorts though.

16/03/07

I had a nice sleep-n today, didn't do much just the usual gym visit and watched a DVD, we've been discussing where to put our bottled water as someone has stolen eighteen cases of water out of our villa while we were on the Al Asad trip. We're going to ASP 7 and ASP 8 tomorrow, then on Monday we're off back up to Al Asad and Camp Wolf so a busy day on Monday.

I absolutely hate travelling along the Uranium road, it's so boring and you get bumped all over the place because the roads are so bad. Well at least time will go quicker towards leave if we're out and busy.

17/03/07

A lovely calm day again today and we made good time driving to ASP 7 and 8, although on the way back up the North Tampa road we came across the freshly burnt out shell of an Aegis Land Cruiser that had been hit by an IED. We weren't sure if anyone was killed but no doubt we'll find out tomorrow. It's a day off tomorrow so I'll give our vehicle a check over before the Al Asad run on Monday.

18/03/07

Our team had a fast ball today as they had to go out to Camp Victory as Chris (manager) needed a lift. I stayed behind to get my armoured vehicle repaired and get it ready for tomorrow's journey up north to Camp Wolf and Al Asad. We have got to take one Parson's client up to Camp Wolf so at least we're taking no trucks so it'll be a fast run tomorrow only thing is there has been a lot of IEDs on the route we're taking so we'll need to keep our eyes open.

19/03/07

We had a nice surprise today when we went to the Farm we found out that another PSD team had already taken our client to

Al Asad so we had the day off. We will be taking an enquiry team to ASP 8 tomorrow so they can do a full investigation into the area where Don was killed and how it happened. I think they will be interviewing a number of people from ASP 8 as well. Baz said we will be staying overnight and coming back on Wednesday.

We have been informed that the insurgents are starting to use dirty bombs. They are filling gas bottles with a powder chemical which burns the skin. It's just over three weeks away to leave and I can't wait, me and the guys have already started to get excited. I will miss the guys on leave as the team has built a strong bond. It's always hard trying to explain to someone from back home as they don't understand what you go through out here, unlike the guys I work with, we're all on the same level.

20/03/07

We took the EOD investigation team down to ASP 8 today so that they could finalise their report on how Don was killed while handling ordnance. We thought we would be staying overnight but they finished early, we had a slow fifty mph drive down and the same going back although we had no trouble.

I found out today that Marcus and Dave may be leaving the team to go and do static guard at one of the ASPs mind it doesn't surprise me as the guys are getting tired of being messed around and not knowing what task they're on next, but in this job you've got to be flexible. They have to realise that there are guys waiting to jump into their shoes and fresh out of the army, they're only too glad to come and earn the money, if only they knew the true risks they'll be taking though.

The EOD investigation team and some of the guys taking a break at Scania on route to ASP 8.

Baz briefing the guys at ASP 8 just before we leave for Baghdad.

21/03/07

Had a day off today so got to do some training, the rest of the boys were feeling the effects of driving slow yesterday and most stayed in bed late this morning. We've got a local job tomorrow as we're off into the green zone to do a recce on a pick-up point where we have to collect the general of the EOD corps on the 1st April.

Found out that the insurgent bombers have stooped to all time low-levels of scummery, they are using children. The bombers are pulling up to checkpoints with the car filled with explosives and children in the car, the insurgent then walks off, leaving the car to the unsuspecting soldier at the checkpoint who thinks nothing can be wrong as children are in the car. Little does the soldier know the children get blown up with the car, how they can justify that — lambs to the slaughter I'd say.

22/03/07

We did the recce today at the green zone and got a view of where we would be collecting the general, this will help things to run smooth on the day. We also went to collect water today then called at the 'Crossed Swords' to take a team photo; it's hard to believe that Saddam Hussein actually stood there many times while his army paraded past.

I remember seeing him on the news stood with a gun, shooting it in the air as vehicles passed carrying Scud missiles, it's said that the hands holding the swords were sculpted from Saddam's own hands. We will be going to Al Asad tomorrow but have to call at Ramadi first. A team have been stuck there for a few days after being attacked, I think they had some casualties.

It was the team that was going to take our client to Al Asad a couple of days ago; it could have easily been us who were attacked.

Well, hopefully it will be quiet on the way up tomorrow and we should make good time as none of our clients are EOD Health and Safety, so foot to the floor. We heard a loud bang today while we were sunbathing on the roof it was pretty close and I must admit it did make me jump; it'll probably be on the news later saying how many people the bomb killed. I think it was probably a VBIED (Vehicle Bomb Improvised Explosive Device) they're nasty as you don't know the bomb is there until it's too late.

Team 46 in all its glory at the 'Crossed Swords' Baghdad.

Saddam Hussein's parade area.

23/03/07

We got news about Kev today, as Mike from Team 45 visited him while he was on leave, Kev will never be the same again. Kev has had a third of his skull removed and had a platinum plate in its place, he has lost forty pounds in weight and is unable to hold a conversation. Kev knows he was in Iraq but still doesn't know what happened and is still unaware that an IED (Improvised Explosive Device) blew his hatch down on his head.

It's times when you hear how one of the lads has truly suffered, when you really start reconsidering your future career options and how long do you gamble with your life. I hope Kev improves and his life will come to some form of normality, however the mental scars will be there for the rest of his life.

We had a quiet run up to Camp Duhlab today although we heard a couple of shots fired near Ramadi. We waited at Camp Duhlab for about three hours while Jacky and Murray from Parson's EOD attended a meeting we then made our way to Al Asad. I hope I get a good night's sleep tonight but I've taken precautions and got my ear plugs on standby in case Baz lets rip with his snoring. Off to Camp Wolf tomorrow just up the road from here then back down to Baghdad.

24/03/07
Woke up to bad weather this morning, Jacky and Murray (EODT Managers) Corps of Engineers were going to inspect the accommodation of the EODT personnel at Camp Wolf. They're looking for illegal weapons, alcohol and pornographic films which are strictly prohibited under the contract they signed.

The inspection took longer than expected and became quite hostile at times and Jacky thought he may have needed us to calm things but it soon settled without our intervention. We didn't finish at Camp Wolf until four p.m. so we had to stay another night at Al Asad which isn't too bad as the internet is good and we get another cooked meal. On the way back from Camp Wolf it started to rain and became hazy and the redness in the sky made the area look like a Martian landscape.

The rain is full of dust out here and falls more like mud balls than rain water, it reminded me of the brown snowflakes in Afghanistan when I was in Gardez. We're leaving early in the morning for Baghdad so we get back early hopefully it'll be a smooth run and we don't get any hold-ups on the way.

Jacky (EODT Manager).

Murray (EODT Manager).

25/03/07

It was a relaxed start this morning, although Baz was slightly pissed off with Ray for not refuelling his vehicle the evening before. The last thing you want to do is keep a client waiting, time is important and the smallest of things can cause a domino effect through the whole day. After Baz had a quiet word with the guys, we left Al Asad and made our way down Uranium my favourite road (NOT).

We had been told prior to us leaving that a US Humvee vehicle had detonated a PIED, all four soldiers inside were injured but luckily none were killed. As we drove past the area where the Humvee was bombed still burning as we passed, we noticed a fuel tanker that had also detonated a PIED. It surprises me how the insurgents can place the bombs so effectively on a military only road and the only other people that use it are the civilian security contractors like us.

After we had got to the end of Uranium, we passed through the US military checkpoint, I noticed they had increased their armour presence there as there were a lot more tanks parked up. Our journey back down to Baghdad was good and we made good time and didn't run into any difficulties on the way.

When I got back to the Villas, I went down the gym to do some training and bumped into Martyn, who I know from back home in Ystradgynlais. He said he was hit bad last week by an IED in Mushada and his vehicle was destroyed, his two gunners the driver and himself had to spend the day in hospital to be checked over. Luckily, they were given the all clear, Martyn said it was a complex attack and the insurgents also used RPGs

(Rocket Propelled Grenades) and machine gun fire at their convoy.

It was nice to see Martyn in one piece but the reality of the incident hit home with him as he told me, "I can't wait to get out of this shit hole and go on leave." (Can't we all). We're out on a local job tomorrow then hopefully a day or two off again before we go back up to Al Asad but my happy thoughts are on leave which is only two and half weeks away now.

Ashes and smoke marking the area on Uranium where the Humvee and fuel tanker detonated the PIED.

Extra armour at the checkpoint at the end of Route Uranium.

26/03/07

It was a local job today as we only had to take two clients into the green zone and then take them back to Camp Victory. While we were in the green zone, Baz mentioned the generals visit on the 1st April which is a high priority job, I asked who would be the PPOs (Personal Protection Officers) for his visit. Baz said it would be Cammy and Mick, I was a bit surprised at this as I think only Mick has done a valid CP course (close protection) as this is relevant to what actions to take if something goes wrong.

Although the green zone is quite secure there is still a lot of Iraqis travelling in the area, but it's Baz's call at the end of the day, so if he is happy then we have to go with it. We haven't got any jobs on now until the 1st of April so a well-deserved couple of days off and a nice long sleep-in tomorrow.

27/03/07

Felt a little worse for wear this morning as I had a few nightcaps last night while I was on messenger talking to pals. I just took it easy today but still managed to get a training session in, there were loud bangs from the US artillery guns in the green zone again today, so someone somewhere is getting a pounding.

The guys on my rotation are starting to feel the buzz of leave now, as am I, can't wait to get on the plane. The villa is starting to feel like the *Big Brother* house now but without the cameras, it's the way it is when you live under each other's feet for so long but we've learnt to get along. Another day off tomorrow unless we get a fast ball but I've heard nothing off Baz as of yet so we'll have to wait and see.

28/03/07

Not much to write about today as it was another chilled day today, we got to go down to the Farm at Camp Victory on Friday to clean the vehicles and check them over before the high-profile job on the 1st April. We still haven't heard any news on future missions yet but we soon know when we're out.

29/03/07

Had a little admin to sort out with the vehicles today and we sorted out all the ammo and pyrotechnics. In total our team has 17,000 rounds of ammunition, thirty smoke grenades, ten phosphorous grenades used to burn immobilised vehicles, ten flash bangs and around twenty flares. We distributed all the ammo and pyro between all the vehicles, it's best to have too much than too little as you never know how long you could be in a fire-fight for.

I had a look at Derrick's bright idea today, he's had an ammo box welded to the gun arm where the Minimi machine gun is mounted. The problem with this is obvious, the weight of the ammo will make the gun arm tilt to one side and the plate that's fitted to the arm is so big you can't rotate the gun. Well you can't tell people anything if they're not going to listen to you and it's too late when the bullets are flying.

We're off to Camp Victory tomorrow to wash all the vehicles before the weekend high profile job; it also gives us the chance to get some things from the PX.

The lads getting stuck into sorting the ammunition out.

Cammy drying and cleaning the Minimi chain ammunition in belts of two hundred rounds of 5.56mm.

30/03/07

We got our vehicles washed today and got a good bit of shopping done, so I should be OK until I go on leave. We've got a job tomorrow into the green zone, I think it will be to do with the general's visit, but I can't see the job running too late.

The internet has finally come on after being down for two days as it had crashed. Some bright spark from the PC department thought they would put a higher firewall setting on the net except it was stopping everyone from opening their e-mails and finally caused the system to crash. I'm not looking forward to the job on Sunday when we take the general down to ASP 8, its going to be a nice steady 50mph, brilliant, well at least we got our $400 monthly spending money today.

31/03/07

It went well today and although there was a lot of hanging around, the general was pleased with how the team operated and how professional we were. He had a Cochise security team the last time he visited and said they were more suitably dressed to go down the beach than to do security, they had shorts on and bandanas on their heads.

We took the general to two meetings in the green zone today and then took him back to the Farm. We have an early start tomorrow and will be leaving the villas for 5.30 a.m. so we can get to ASP 8 nice and early. I hope it's just another quiet run down south as we usually get, hopefully all our jobs up until we go on leave will be quiet runs.

01/04/07

Well, it's April Fool's Day today although nobody planned any silly surprises, we took two US military colonels to ASP 8 to inspect the site. The journey was agony, just doing 50mph, it's so mind-numbing and a few of the lads were nodding off not that it's their fault it's a stupid speed and we really shouldn't be driving that slow.

Our journey went well today and after we had a well earnt meal at the de-frac, we went back to the Villas.

02/04/07

We picked up two clients up from the green zone this morning. They were two members of the enquiry team investigating the accident down at ASP 8. Their final meeting would give the full report on how Don was killed by the artillery shell at ASP 8. We found out later in the day that an Aegis team were IEDd as they left the green zone after we did this morning, fortunately there were no casualties.

I got an interesting e-mail this morning from one of my mates about the chlorine bombs, it's pretty interesting.

Suicide Truck Bomb Captured in Ramadi

RAMADI, IRAQ (March 24, 2007) –Iraqi Police apprehended a suicide truck bomber and captured his vehicle, containing a large quantity of chlorine and explosives, when it failed to detonate in Ramadi, March 23.

A white cargo truck filled with chlorine and explosive failed to detonate in Ramadi.

At approximately 1.30 p.m., a white cargo truck came to a halt near the entrance to the Jezeera police station, located about 150 meters from a water treatment plant. The police approached the truck for further investigation and detained the driver when they discovered the truck was rigged with explosives and the driver was attempting to detonate the vehicle.

Upon further investigation, the truck contained an unknown number of fifty-five-gallon drums, which were used to camouflage five one thousand-gallon barrels filled with chlorine and more than two tons of explosives.

The truck cargo area reveals containers filled with chlorine and explosives. The truck failed to detonate and was seized by Jezeera police in Ramadi.

The driver is being held for further questioning and all explosives were removed from the truck and destroyed by demolition experts.

03/03/07

We took ten Armor Group personnel to Al Asad today; they will be replacing the ten EODT security guys that have been sacked at Camp Wolf, due to weapon and drinking offences. Armor has won the static guard security contract at Camp Wolf so at least the guys will have work for some time.

Our journey up to Al Asad was quiet and the roads had a spooky silence as there were hardly any vehicles traveling on the roads around Fallujah or Ramadi. There were some shots fired on Uranium but they weren't aimed in our direction so there were no worries. Tomorrow we'll collect the ten EODT guys from Camp Wolf then make our way back down to Baghdad. They aren't going to be in a good mood as they'll all be looking for new jobs so I'll keep the chit chat to a minimum.

04/04/07

Well, the ear plugs were in last night but I was so tired I would have been deaf to the world anyway. We collect the bad boys from Camp Wolf and head straight down Uranium, we bumped into two convoys but weren't held up for too long. We carried on to the end of Uranium and had our usual break then head off for route Mobile.

The run down Mobile was quiet and I said to Cammy we have been fortunate to have had quiet runs lately. We had no trouble at Ramadi, Fallujah or Abu Ghraib and as a result we made Baghdad in good time. We have got the next two days off so time to chill and do some admin and wait for the next task.

Cammy and Baz counting how many trucks pass us on Uranium, I think he lost count.

05/04/07

We had a brief at eleven a.m. this morning and Baz went through some points with us, he also mentioned something a bit concerning. He said the insurgents are using teenagers to throw IEDs at the military and contract security teams. The children always run up to vehicles asking for food and water so noticing whether they are going to throw something is going to be difficult and, unfortunately, if they do throw an IED they will be treated like an insurgent and shot.

A thirteen-year-old threw an IED into the turret of an American military armoured vehicle last week so we will need to be more cautious from now on. We also talked about the vehicle spacing, on Uranium I agree we should space in case a large IED takes two vehicles out. On the motorways, it's different but everyone had their own view, especially Dave, he was in a world of his own and his driving is something not to be desired.

People should concentrate on their own professionalism instead of how other people do their jobs, far too many people in the team think they do everything right — how wrong they are.

06/04/07

We took half of our team down to the Farm today as they'll be joining Team 45 for the next three days. They'll be going to ASP 7 and ASP 8 then up to Camp Duhlab so they must be escorting trucks. They should be back on Tuesday then on Wednesday we will have one more mission up to Camp Ramadi and Camp Michigan then straight back to Baghdad.

After our mission on Wednesday, we will be getting ready to leave on Thursday, we'll clean weapons and pack boxes and be ready to go on leave.

07/04/07

Quiet day today, nothing much happened just went down to the Farm to collect one of the Excursion vehicles ready for our mission on Tuesday. Weather was blurry today, more dust and sand in the air than anything but no rain. We're just on the home straight now and can't wait to go on leave. did some packing tonight so I'd have less to do next week.

08/04/07

Just another quiet day in the villa today, I made sure my going home clothes were washed ready. We have heard the guys who went to join Team 45 are still stuck at the Farm as Team 45's vehicles have broken down, so the missions will be put back. Got tomorrow off and then out on our final mission on Tuesday up to Ramadi and Camp Michigan.

09/04/07

Not much to write about only a lot of demonstrations about the US occupation of Iraq today. There have been a few bombs going off but nothing to close to the villas. Off on the job to Ramadi and Camp Michigan tomorrow, to escort twelve EODT guys, so I hope it's a quiet journey before we go on leave.

10/04/07

The journey up to Camp Michigan was quiet this morning and we got there in about two hours. You couldn't call it a camp really as there was a lot of construction to do, that's why we had so many people to take up, most were Philippine workers who would be driving the machinery and doing manual labour. After we dropped the people off, we then made our way back down Route Mobile to Baghdad.

We called in Camp Ramadi on the way back, which was a mistake as the US military wouldn't let us leave the camp unless we were escorted. We got back to Camp Victory at around 3.30 p.m. then made our way back to the Villas.

Team 45 vehicles and ours parked on the area of ground where Camp Michigan will be built.

Team 43 arriving with their convoy mostly, machinery and equipment for the new camp.

Workers starting to off-load the machinery to begin the ground work.

11/04/07

Well, I just had a quiet relaxing day today before I fly out to Dubai tomorrow. I handed my weapons into the armoury with the rest of the guys then emptied all my ammunition from my magazines. I've packed my kit for going home and boxed my work kit so nothing else to do now except watch a good film.

Cammy cooked a lovely lasagne and did some garlic bread, which was appreciated, so I'm feeling quite cosy now.

10/05/07

Well, back in the sun with my gun and, believe it or not, I was quite glad to get back as the enjoyment of leave starts to wear off by the fourth week. The normality of everyone's life back home makes me realise what type of work I do and how different my life is from the people I went to school with.

Well just sorting out our vehicle as I'm gunner, partnered with Cammy and Chris and to get back into it a lovely run up north to Camp Sommerall so may have some action in Mushada.

11/05/07

Did a bit of shopping today, as we went in to the IZ then Camp Victory so we called at the PX. Our vehicle has been left in a shit state by the other lads, so we'll give it a clean out tomorrow before Sunday's job.

15/05/07

I've decided to only put relevant things that aren't so monotonous in my diary, as some days just aren't worth writing about. Well the quiet runs down south changed today and even after having a mission up north over the last few days we had no trouble but today, that changed. After taking four clients down to ASP 8 we made our way back up Tampa south towards Baghdad.

I, PPO (Personal Protection Officer), Cammy, (Driver) and Chris, (Vehicle Commander) were in the Excursion vehicle travelling between Brown 7 and 8 which are route markers just outside Baghdad. Cammy had just put the radio on when boom, an IED had been detonated opposite our vehicle on the left by the central reservation, so the insurgents obviously thought we were still carrying clients. The flash from the blast was right next to Cammy's driver's window and all of our ears were ringing from the loud bang, but unbelievably the vehicle suffered no major damage, just a few scratches.

It was strange as I brought my hands up as if to protect myself when the bomb went off, we all laughed after, as more to appreciate that we were still alive after someone had tried to kill us although I could see the paleness in Cammy's face as shock set in. Chris and I joked as it was the second time we had been hit by an IED and the fact that we all jumped out of our seats. Well, we are all here to fight another day with smiles on our faces but the thought always lingers about the next time we get hit, will the IED be bigger or smaller, more effective or less effective who can tell.

20/05/07 — The Longest day.

We were given a task today to collect seven clients from Camp Fallujah, so we presumed it would be a quick task but Shane said he had a gut feeling something was going to happen. The seven clients had been stuck there for a couple of days due to one of their vehicles breaking down. We arrived at Camp Fallujah at around 08.45 a.m. and were told to wait by the front gate until we had clearance to enter the camp, it was at that point I heard Baz call Shane over the radio, "Quick mate, I need to you."

Before I knew it, we were driving back east the way we had come, Shane came over the radio and explained what was happening. He said that Team 42 had been hit and that ops (Operations Room) could not get in contact with them and could we go and assist them. On our way there, we all knew we would be coming into trouble and hearts started to race with anticipation, I couldn't have imagined what I was about to come into. As we approached Team 42, we could see they were under attack from insurgents from the right-hand side but my attention was gripped by the sight of a mangled armoured vehicle with bodies lying around it.

The team had been escorting a convoy of recovery trucks to Camp Fallujah when their rear vehicle was hit by the largest IED I had ever seen, the insurgents had filled a drainage pipe full of explosives. The pipe ran the length of the motorway, so there was a hole right across the six lanes. My first reaction was to get the med bag and go and help as I was the Excursion commander with no clients to protect, I could leave the vehicle.

I took a quick glance at Chris and Cammy and jumped out and ran in the direction of the mangled vehicle noticing the crack of the odd bullet or two overhead as I ran. I glanced back and noticed Cammy had exited the Excursion and had taken up a fire position at the rear of one of the flat-bed trucks.

When I got to the vehicle, I could see the extent of the carnage that the bomb had caused, I immediately saw Martyn, he had just placed a tourniquet on one of the Fijian lads who had his left arm severed by the pod roof. I looked at the top of the vehicle where I could see the Fijians severed arm perched there under some debris. I grabbed the arm and put it in our drinks cool box, normally used to keep our bottled water cool. I checked the second casualty quickly so we could get them in the vehicles, the second Fijian was breathing and conscious so we lifted him in to Baz's vehicle. During this, I was constantly aware of bullets cracking above our heads.

The Fijian who had lost his arm was put into Shane's vehicle so he could be taken quickly to the Fallujah med centre. After the worse casualties had been put in vehicles, Shane and I took up fire positions near the front of Baz's vehicle to put some covering fire down for Aaron (Team 42 2i/c) and Chris's (Team 42 Team Leader) team, as they were trying to protect the truck drivers. Everything seemed to last forever but I knew things were happening quickly and I had soon gone from twelve magazines of ammunition down to two.

I had gone through three hundred and sixty rounds of ammunition, so I quickly grabbed some spare mags from Baz's vehicle, passing two or three to Shane. I looked up and saw Shane firing over the front of Baz's vehicle, when suddenly I saw him quickly move back as if he'd been hit in the face. I rushed over to Shane and asked him to look at me. I could see he was bleeding from the mouth at this point I immediately thought the worst and that he'd been shot in the face. A small fragment of the bullet had ricochet off the bonnet of the vehicle and gone through Shane's cheek and lodged itself in his throat, I asked him if he was OK and he replied he was. I could only describe Shane as being like a kid in a sweet shop and he was enjoying getting stuck into the insurgents and there wasn't anything going to stop him.

I could see Sammy and Andy exiting their vehicle to my right and almost spontaneously they opened fire on the insurgents, our top gunners by now had gone through a thousand rounds of ammunition each. I ran over to Sammy's vehicle and took up a fire position at the front of the vehicle. I then asked Nick (pod gunner) to give me some smoke grenades so I could make a smoke screen to give us some more cover. Sammy did well to manoeuvre his vehicle to give Andy and I cover as we went back for Shane who was near one of the flat-bed trucks. I glanced in the direction of where the insurgents were firing from, a small gap in the reeds on our right about four hundred metres away by a muddy bank. I could see movement and quickly fired some short bursts of two or three rounds at the images in front of me, one seemed to fall heavily to the ground but this only made me more committed to my aim.

At this point, the barrel of my weapon was getting way to hot and was causing my weapon to jam as the odd round was getting stuck in the breach, so I had to manually cock the rifle. We continued firing into the area where the insurgents were firing from, so much so that the long reeds caught fire but we were still taking gunfire from their direction so they must have been dug in well. We continued the fire fight for around thirty minutes until a US marines came in Humvees with 50mm calibre machine guns; they started firing to give us cover so we could extract everyone out of the line of fire.

Shane and I were the last to get off the ground into Baz's vehicle. The casualties had already left, we were all buzzing from the rush of adrenalin, as we drove back Shane shook my hand and said, well done mate. It was a good feeling though, knowing we had all worked well together and recovered the team successfully without anyone being killed. My trousers were covered in blood and were torn during the fire fight but I didn't really notice.

Out of the attack, three Fijians were injured and Aaron, who was in a good condition considering what he had been through, and Shane with the face and throat injury. Unfortunately, the doctors were unable to re-connect the Fijians left arm after we had found it on top of the armoured vehicle. When we arrived back in Baghdad, it was confirmed that two civilians were killed and one injured in the crossfire.

After a search was conducted by the US marines in the area of the reeds, they found two insurgents dead and two seriously injured, mind, with all the firepower going in their direction I'm surprised two survived. At the end of the day, none of either team was killed and we live to fight another day. The guys did well today and showed true camaraderie.

The armoured vehicle facing west with the motorway ripped up.

What's left of the cab.

Bloodstained Pod where Fijian gunner lost his arm.

All six lanes of the motorway blown up.

Front view of armoured vehicle.

Drainage pipe running under motorway where explosives were placed.

View of motorway with burning reeds in background where insurgents were positioned.

One of the flat-bed trucks leaking oil after the gun battle.

I was just about to collect Aaron's equipment from the cab, his Ipod was in one piece.

Truck driver killed in crossfire.

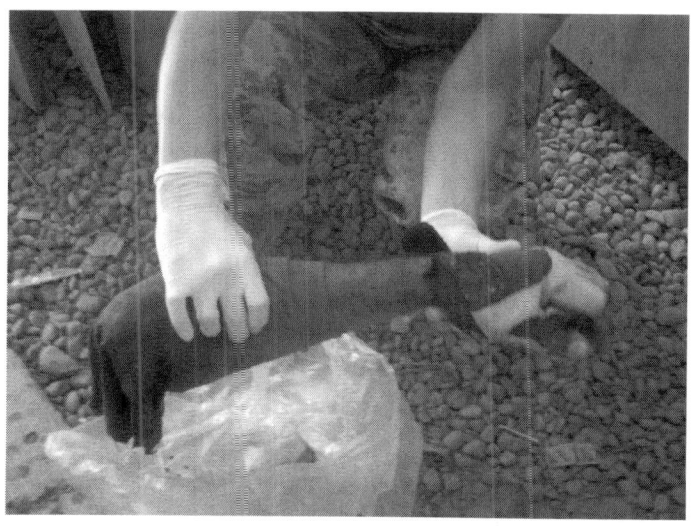

Fijians severed arm.

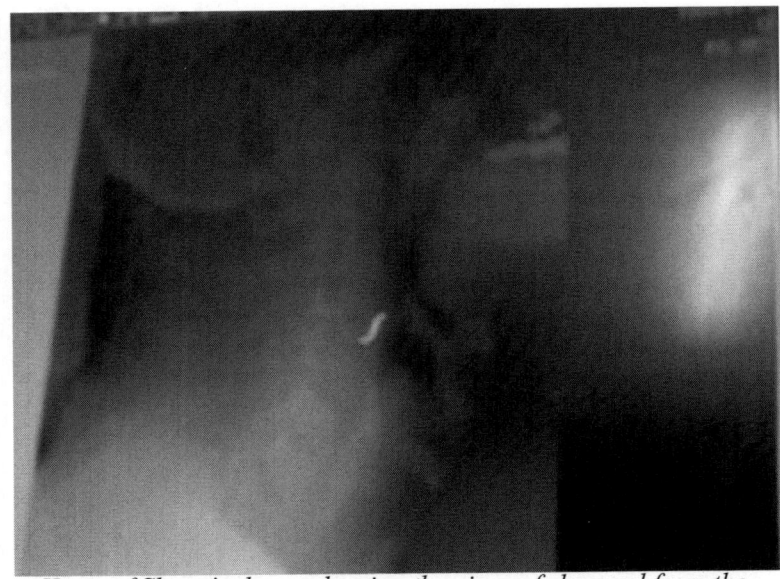

X-ray of Shane's throat showing the piece of shrapnel from the bullet.

10/06/07 — A Bridge Too Far.

I thought today would have been another regular run down to ASP 8 but the return journey would prove otherwise. We were taking some VIP clients down for a visit, these included Colonel Bush, who is one of the main people of Parsons, and members of Associated Press. After the EODT team had done a controlled explosion for the visitors we left ASP 8 and head back down route Kiev to route Tampa.

We had got to about one hundred and twenty kilometres south of Baghdad when we saw an enormous cloud of smoke about a kilometre in front of us, a few seconds later the shockwave hit us. The blast was huge and we knew it must have been an IED or something. As we approached the clearing smoke, we couldn't believe our eyes, the US checkpoint that was on the bridge had been destroyed and the right side of the bridge had collapsed.

The checkpoint had been hit by a VBIED (Vehicle Born Improvised Explosive Device) and had been detonated by the right side support pillars of the bridge. Immediately we could see that the soldiers needed help, at which point Baz gave us the order to stop and assist. Cammy exited the excursion vehicle with the med pack and went to assist the casualties, while I stayed with the clients on the main road.

The bridge was unstable and could have collapsed at any time but the guys had to try and rescue the injured. Ray, Chris Powell, John, Marcus and Baz went to where the large area of rubble was. They managed to get four injured soldiers from the rubble by improvising and using one of the US tanks and vehicle straps to pull large slabs of concrete off the injured soldiers, unfortunately three were killed due to being crushed by the concrete. I ensured the photographer didn't get too close as I knew he would have taken pictures of the injured soldiers and that's the last thing their parents and family need to see on the news. I've put the news report below which was written by the reporter travelling in my vehicle during the bomb incident.

MAHMOUDIYA, Iraq — An apparent suicide car bomber took aim at a US convoy carrying demolition experts on Sunday, collapsing a major highway overpass south of Baghdad and trapping American soldiers in the rubble.

The vehicle detonated beside a support pillar, bringing down an army checkpoint and a tent that had been on the collapsing span, dubbed 'Checkpoint 20' by the US military. The overpass, one of two crossing over Iraq's main north-south highway in the region, appeared to be closed to all but military traffic at the time.

A US army quick reaction force and the staff of Armor Group International, a private security firm that was in charge of the passing convoy, worked for some forty-five minutes to pull trapped men from the rubble about six miles east of Mahmoudiya.

There appeared to be several casualties, including an Iraqi interpreter who was wounded, according to Donald Campbell, an official with the security firm who was at the scene.

The attack, which was witnessed by an Associated Press reporter and a photographer who were in the approaching convoy, occurred in the triangle of death, so called for frequent Sunni insurgent attacks.

On May 12, three US soldiers were captured in an ambush near Mahmoudiya that left five other soldiers, including an Iraqi dead. An al-Qaida front group the Islamic State of Iraq issued a video last week claiming the three missing troops had been killed, but the US military said it would not accept that and was continuing with its search.

Iraqi police said the overpass was a vital link across the highway for villagers in the area because the other spans have been taken over by US forces. A police officer in nearby Iskandariyah, speaking on condition of anonymity because of security concerns, said a curfew had been imposed on vehicles and pedestrians after the attack on the span and earlier bombings of a mosque and a Sunni political party's headquarters that caused some damage but no casualties.

As we're about to approach the checkpoint moments after the explosion.

Cloud of smoke covers the area.

Our first view of the damage as we arrive at the checkpoint, the whole area is covered with debris and shrapnel from the blast the vehicle itself had totally disintegrated.

Soldiers in shock after the blast looking for their comrades.

Les, Cammy and Ray give medical aid and assist soldiers to rescue the trapped and injured.

Me doing the role of PPO (Personal Protection Officer) for Colonel Bush, photographer and Associated Press Member.

Medivac Blackhawk helicopter landing on Tampa in front of Baz's vehicle.

Second Medivac helicopter coming in to land.

US Soldiers prepare to move casualty into helicopter.

First injured US soldier is placed on the Medivac helicopter.

12/06/07 — E-mail from complete stranger to AGI.

After the bridge incident an e-mail was sent by someone to Armor Group International, below is what the e-mail said.

Message:

My name is Christopher Whitehead and I live in the United States. Last week I was watching a special about Soldiers of Fortune in Iraq on the National Geographic Channel. They talked about Armor Group International and what you do over in Iraq. I saw on the news today that a suicide truck bomber blew up a bridge in Baghdad. The same time this happened a convoy under the protection of Armor Group came by. Your employees rushed over to help the 3rd Infantry Division to secure the site and help rescue the trapped soldiers. I just want to say thank you. Please don't take this the wrong way, but the world needs a few more cowboys.

Sincerely, Chris Whitehead.

Well it's nice to know we get appreciated by the public and not all comments are about why we are here and should we be doing the job we do. Comments above truly make the job worthwhile.

18/06/07

After the incident with Team 42, the Culvert IED and ambush and the suicide bridge bomb at the US military checkpoint I have noticed a significant bond in our team. Yes, we have our moans about one another but doesn't any good marriage have its ups and downs. It is surprising though how experiencing these major events and being there for one another brings a team together and gives you confidence in one another.

We all have bonded and have become a stronger team as we know we all can do the job when it matters the most. It makes it a pleasure to work alongside men you can rely on through thick and thin.

07/09/07 — The Loss of a comrade.

This morning, half of our team joined Team 45 to go on a mission to ASP 8, Lez, Paul, Lee, Marcus, John, Cheese and Ray, as their convoy turned onto route Kiev about eight kilometres from ASP 8 one of the PLS trucks was EFPd. The driver of the PLS was Daren and the passenger was Ray, the EFP hit the passenger side of the PLS truck spinning the vehicle; this caused severe injuries to Ray.

The other team members went to assist the guys in the PLS but found Ray had lost an arm and leg in the explosion while Darren had suffered a broken leg and some cuts. Unfortunately, by the time the guys had got Ray into one of the armoured vehicles he had lost a significant amount of blood and by the time the team had got back to ASP 8, Ray had died.

The team will be bringing Ray's body back tomorrow and then his body will be sent to Kuwait where it will be flown home. Ray was a quiet character when first joining Team 46 last October but since the suicide bridge bombing, where he played an essential role in rescuing three American soldiers, he had come out of his shell and was quite a humorous person at times. Only yesterday, he was one of six of our team who had been presented with a bravery award from the Royal Humane Society.

He will be missed by his fellow team members but mostly our thoughts will be with his girlfriend and family in Tandragee, County Armagh. This sad incident makes us realise that we are always in harm's way and never know when the swift hand of fate will tap us on the shoulder, only the choices we make dictates what path we take in our lives and what the future will bring good or bad.

Ray will be missed by us all.

Ray (left) and his previous vehicle partner John (right).

10/11/07

Charmaine said to me on the phone today, "Don't be upset, Dad," and God did she sound old, but it was nice to hear her comforting words.

Nico surprised me though, as he was asking for me to come home, he is so familiar with the danger out here and he is only seven years old and totally aware his dad is in a dangerous place. He said, "Dad, can't you find a job back home that isn't so dangerous so I can see you, can you come back now because I miss you dad." His words were like a spear through my heart and I know he was talking reason but he is unaware of what holds me to do this work and why I like the job I do as it flows in my blood.

We were told this morning that Colin, from Team 45, was killed near Basra while escorting a convoy on the AOL contract. He had recently transferred from Team 45 to convoys. The risks are higher on convoys but the pay is higher and even though we all know the risks we are still willing to gamble our lives. We were told Colin was killed by an EFP, I just hope he didn't suffer, and it was over quickly.

17/11/07 — Bang On

Yesterday, we took three clients up north to Camp Sommerall, the journey up there was quiet and without incident even though we were warned there is still a lot of insurgent activity in the Mushada area. We had a casual afternoon and stayed overnight which was a welcoming treat as we wouldn't have to cook back at the Villa's and it meant we could have a decent shower.

This morning we got ready early and left for Baghdad at around 08.00 hours, we would make good time along as we had a trouble-free run but that wasn't going to be Shane (TL) was in Alpha lead vehicle then Nick driving Charlie vehicle then me driving Delta and Baz (2i/c) bringing up the rear in Bravo. The journey was going well, even through Samara, things were quiet and I thought we would make good time for Baghdad.

We were driving through Mushada at around 10.00 hours when our lead vehicle was stopped by an ING (Iraqi National Guard) Humvee, Shane came over the radio and said the ING soldier had said there was an IED just round the corner. The soldier mentioned something about the left hand side but I was uncertain whether he meant the IED was on the left or that the Insurgents were on the left. Shane set off with caution and manoeuvred his vehicle over to the left hand lane, we began go round the corner, I noticed there were no vehicles on our lane or on the opposite side. The road straightened out when all of a sudden there was a flash and thump from a shockwave of a large explosion in front of my vehicle, Charlie vehicle had been hit by the IED and it was bang on. I heard Nick come over the radio, "I've been immobilised."

I couldn't see a thing as the explosion had caused a dust and smoke screen in front of me but I kept on driving through, pushing left slightly to avoid the IED crater expecting to see the Charlie vehicle in pieces. To my surprise the Charlie vehicle was undamaged except for the engine; I couldn't see John on the Charlie rear gun so I was hoping he was OK, I noticed there was fluid pouring out of the Charlie vehicle's engine. Charlie vehicle was slowly losing speed at which point I came up behind Nick's vehicle in order to push him out of the kill zone. It wasn't easy to see where I was pushing the Charlie vehicle so I manoeuvred left slightly to get a better view. I accelerated and brought both vehicles up to 50 mph it seemed a little crazy but I knew we couldn't hang around and it was the right thing to do.

I kept pushing Nick's vehicle until we came to the next ING checkpoint where Paul and Nick put a pull bar on the Charlie vehicle as the engine had been totally blown by the blast.

It was comforting to know that our armoured vehicles could take a direct hit from a blast and protect the occupants and that's the most important thing everyone, was OK. After Nick and Sammy had replaced the front tyres, we set off for Baghdad again where Shane's vehicle would tow Charlie to the Villa's instead of finishing at Camp Victory. Well, we know we can't always have a quiet run but if we can't have a trouble free run we can still have a safe one with everyone OK so we start as a team and finish as a team.

Sammy changing the damaged tyre on the Charlie vehicle after the IED blast, scorch marks from the blast visible on the front of the vehicle.

23/11/07

Well, this morning was not its usual quiet moment in front of the television watching the news while having a cup of tea. I heard a commotion outside the front of the villa so Gary, Baz and I went outside to see what was wrong, when we got there we could see three dogs attacking a cat. Doughy and another two dogs were ripping a cat to pieces and the poor thing hadn't a chance, Gary and I chased the dogs off the cat but it was seriously hurt.

I noticed the dogs had broken the cat's pelvis and it had no use of its back legs, the dogs had gone at it a few times and the cat was in a bad way. There was only one option as the cat was in terrible pain and would not be able to survive through the day; it would be more humane to kill the cat than let the dogs finish it off. Greg held the cat down with a broom as I give it a swift blow to the back of the head with a piece of wood and then I put its body into a plastic bag so it could be disposed.

After I spoke to Baz about my concerns about having the dogs lingering by our villa and the repercussions we could have if the dogs were to attack one of the small children living next door. It felt so strange at the time I killed the cat as I wouldn't even blink to consider shooting and killing an insurgent but felt pity and sorrow for killing the cat, even though it was a mercy killing.

08/02/08 — We're Not The Same As We Used To Be.

Well I haven't made an entry into my diary since before Xmas, probably it's more to do with the fact that there hasn't been much activity over this winter period. My rotation had a good leave especially because it was Xmas and we also had New

Year back home which made it all the more worthwhile. There is a new ASP down south near Basra which means we should be busier in the near future, it's called Atlanta.

I've noticed since Ray's death and the changes that have been in the team we have seemed to have lost the camaraderie we used to have amongst us, this is fuelled by certain individuals who have come to the team. The worst, I feel, is David Cummings who is an ex Welsh Guardsman, he's forty-two, but behaves a lot younger, he is one of those people who seem to know it all and can do it better but, if only that was the truth.

Even though the end of *The Iraq Dairy* has come, the story isn't over as I would have another battle to fight when I get home except the enemy can't be seen, is very close, and can be deadly... PTSD (Post Traumatic Stress Disorder).

This diary was written as it happened. By doing so, I aimed to give the reader, the sense of being there.

A lot of what I saw and experienced in Iraq will never be forgotten and are still in my memories to this day.